COCKNEY RABBIT

A *DICK'N'ARRY*
OF
RHYMING SLANG

Ray Puxley

D0972894

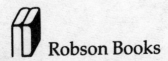

Robson Books

First published in Great Britain in 1992 by Robson Books Ltd, Bolsover House, 5-6 Clipstone Street, London W1P 7EB

Copyright © 1992 Ray Puxley
The right of Ray Puxley to be identified as author of this work has been asserted by him in accordance with the Copyright, Designs and Patents Act 1988

British Library Cataloguing in Publication Data
A catalogue record for this book is available from the British Library

All rights reserved. No part of this publication may be reproduced, stored in a retrieval system, or transmitted in any form or by any means, electronic, mechanical, photocopying, recording or otherwise, without the prior permission in writing of the publishers.

Typeset by Spectrum Typesetters Ltd., London
Printed and bound in Great Britain by Biddles Ltd., Guildford and King's Lynn

Introduction

Much has been written down the years by philologists and socio-linguists, all eminently better qualified than I am to sweep the gutters of the past to trace the origins of a form of speech that was born in them. The most popular belief is that rhyming slang began as a secret language of the underworld, formed in mid-nineteenth century London to confuse the 'peelers' and the casual eavesdropper. That it was used by the roguery of the day is undoubted but it may well have been as contributors rather than founding fathers of rhyming slang.

It has been suggested that the seeds were planted at the beginning of that century during the construction of London's docks. The main work force for this major undertaking were the local men and the immigrants from the Emerald Isle and to perplex their 'foreign' counterparts the Cockneys are said to have invented rhyming slang.

Another theory is that it came from the fertile imaginations of street chanters. These nomadic wanderers would travel from market to market, which at the time were known as fairs, telling stories, reciting ballads and informing the populace of the news. Because there were so many of these itinerant spielers they each had to develop their own style of patter which they did by embellishing it with colourful phrases and pieces of slang. Some of which rhymed.

I have made no attempt to research its history, but what I have endeavoured to do is compile a list of terms that I have heard and used in a lifetime of living and working in London. All the old familiar terms and expressions are included plus many new ones, some of which have been recorded for the first time. Many will be unfamiliar due to the fact that they may be totally regionalized to one area, one pub, one work place or even one person but if it is worthy of inclusion it is here.

A great many new terms have come from the people who have done most to keep the 'Cockney slang' in the public eye. They are the writers who put the clever lines into the mouths of actors, without whom we would not be able to sympathize with Del boy and his 'dodgy Cilla' or buy a 'doppleganger' at the Winchester Club. I have included as many of these as I could keep up with.

Although I have tried not to take the work too seriously I have in some cases pointed out some facts and raised one or two questions. Rhyming slang is, by its nature, a fun thing and is supposed to be light hearted and humorous, which is how I hope it will come across to the reader and why, when asked, I always refer to it as a 'sort of dictionary'. Writers in the past have been quick to protest at the authenticity of certain terms, claiming that since they have not heard them they can't be 'official'. But does that really matter? If a manager of a betting shop wants to refer to his safe as an 'Adam Faith' why shouldn't he? If a beer drinker wants to order a pint of 'Gary Glitter' why not? And I can see no reason why a decorator should not call his paint brush his 'Ian Rush'. As with everything else rhyming slang suffers the ravages of time and these along with other modern examples will, in the future, be replaced by more contemporary counterparts. Who these days tells 'Binnie Hales'? Or drinks 'Ralph Lynn'? Who still plays 'Wilkie Bards'? Or goes on their 'Edna May'? Nobody. Dead people. Dead terms. But like many others their names live on in these pages.

A great number of names included are fictitious, made up solely to effect a rhyme, there are some obvious examples of this. Harry Huggins, Tommy Rollocks, Mrs Duckett etc. Other names, however, are not so evident. Attempts to track down the origins of Joe Hunt, Jim Skinner, Jack Jones and the like have proved futile but it is feasible that these were localized terms of the past that were based on actual people. At least, some of them may have been.

Rhyming slang is a great leveller, the rich and powerful rubbing shoulders with the lowly and everybody treated with equal disrespect. Selina Scott may appear on television with a prince but in this production she appears as an irritation on the nose of a pauper. Dudley Moore may be a very successful comic actor but there is nothing funny abut his role in *Cockney Rabbit*. And the least said about Douglas Hurd, Eartha Kitt and Screamin' Lord Sutch the better. Except to say that no matter what these and others represent it should be taken as a tribute to their fame and they can take comfort in their achievement of a kind of immortality.

Although known as the London slang it is no longer exclusive to the capital. It has been picked up and carried on the air waves of radio and television to the four corners of Britain. Rab C Nesbitt is as likely to give someone a kick up the 'khyber' in Glasgow as Alf Garnet is in Wapping. Indeed the Cockney is no longer confined to London either. As the boundaries of Greater London have expanded to accommodate more and more people, so successive generations of East Enders have spilled over into Essex with Barking, Dagenham and Ilford becoming the new East End. Some have moved further afield to the new towns of Harlow and Basildon and the landlord of a country tavern in Cornwall is as liable to hail from Bow as from Bodmin. And as the people move the language follows, funnelling into new ears and urging new mouths to repeat it.

Most people know a term or two, from dustmen to doctors, from taxi drivers to tax inspectors. Its use these days is in the realm of amusement rather than confusion, with examples being dropped into a conversation for comic effect. As already stated, this was originally the jargon of the lowlife and many of the terms have not risen above ankle level but I have left nothing out on grounds of bad taste and had I omitted examples relating to taboo words, the work would have been considerably shorter. But incomplete.

An important point for the uninitiated is the pronunciation. Rather than write words as they are spoken by Cockneys, which I always think looks corny, I have left it to the reader to do the work and I'll take it for granted that no 'H's will be sounded, 'T's will be flattened, 'TH' will become 'F' in words such as 'thing' and 'mouth' and 'V' in words like 'mother'. Words ending in 'ING' must lose the 'G' and 'OW' becomes 'ER' in 'window', 'shadow' etc.

A lot of terms are inspired by sportsmen, especially those from the horse racing and boxing fraternities. This is totally fitting and highly significant of the importance that both sports played in the lives of East Enders. As a young man my father tried his hand at both boxing and bookmaking so I grew up with tales of the square ring and the silver ring. We heard stories of local fighters who became world champions like Pedlar Palmer, Jack 'Kid' Berg and Teddy Baldock. And tales of men who were never destined for greatness. Men who were forced into the ring to stave off the hand of unemployment; better to have your brains scrambled for two or three quid a fight than nothing. At least you can feed the kids. And sad stories of desperate men, who, in order to boost their meagre wages in their day jobs would turn up at a venue in the hope of being a standby fighter. If somebody on the bill didn't turn up or was unfit to fight, the substitute was in. For this he was paid a small fee and, if it was a good contest, a share of the nobbins (money thrown in by the crowd). No fight, no money. And this after a hard day's work.

There were also great stories of racecourse scams. Of fights with rival 'bookmakers' over the best pitch on Epsom Downs on Derby day. And the tale about the strongly fancied horse that Dad's 'firm' had laid over the odds, who won. But they 'had it over the wall', into a waiting car and were on their way back to London before the race was over. When I was born in 1948 he was a dock worker, so I heard a lot of slang when I was a child.

I made my entry into the world in a hospital in Bow to the loud clanging of bells. Not the famous Bow Bells of course, they are to be found in the church of St Mary-le-Bow in Cheapside a few miles away. My delivery room was directly opposite the hospital bar and I arrived at the same time that they rang the bell for last orders. Apparently this had a terrifying effect on me which would explain the chronic aversion I now have towards closing time.

The fifties was a great time to be a kid especially in Poplar where I grew up. Being near the docks it was a regular target of the Luftwaffe during the Blitz and almost every street bore the scars of that one sided encounter. Vast tracts of rubble strewn wastelands overgrown with a multitude of weeds and wild flowers. And stinging nettles that I swear used to reach out to deliver their spite to the backs of little bare legs. These were our playgrounds. Each child belonged to a gang and every gang had their 'debry' (debris). Most of the time this was fine, there was no real animosity and most of the kids were friends. They played together, members of opposing gangs sat next to each other in school. Then, once a year came the wood war season. This occurred in the week leading up to 5 November, when all gang members would scour the streets for bonfire wood and inter debry rivalry became intense. Now at that time the neighbourhood had a profusion of bombed houses, therefore there was a plentiful supply of wood and other combustibles. But that wasn't good enough. What we had, they wanted and what they had, we had to have. Raids were mounted into 'enemy territory'. This usually happened between five and six o'clock when your scouts came back and reported that all enemy personnel had gone for their teas. There was always a guard but he didn't count because he was always the youngest in the gang. He would stand resolutely at his post, a saucepan on his head and a stick in his hand and a mind full of valour. But at the first sign of a screaming, club wielding bunch of urchins charging towards him he'd be off in the opposite direction to raise the alarm. As if synchronized, nearby doors would open in unison and the opposing army would spill out into the street to begin the battle. Boys would trade blows over a rotted piece of tarpaulin. An old rafter would be the prize in a splintery game of tug o'war. The raiders would eventually retreat taking with them whatever they could. The next night they would be the raided. That's how it was, perfectly good friends would fight each other over a piece of wood that they may have stepped over 365 times since last year.

With no television to keep us in and no traffic to present any danger, the street was everything we needed. It was our football pitch in winter, our cricket pitch in summer (the two seasons never crossed) and our race track. On long summer nights everybody, children and adults would be out, playing, talking, sometimes arguing until it was dark. Those streets are not there anymore, they were pulled down at the end of the sixties to make way for a housing estate. In dreams I often return.

My first ambition was to be a footballer. At eight years old I was told by the school sports master that I had the ability of an eleven year old. Unfortunately, when I was fifteen I still had the ability of an eleven year old. So that was that. At thirteen I got a Saturday job in the new betting shop industry where I was paid the staggering amount of £2.10 shillings (£2.50) for filing away the sloshers (losing bets). Bookmaking, I decided, was a good way to make money so I made a book at school on the 1963 Grand National. This was not a success. The race was won by a 66-1 chance called Ayala and two people backed it. One was a spotty fat kid and the other was the school hard nut from the fifth form who insisted on immediate payment. My pleadings of insolvency were met by my being dangled upside down from a railway bridge. Needless to say I found their money. They bashed me anyway.

With my bookmaking career in ruins I decided to venture into the world of rock 'n'roll. The Beatles and the Stones were in their ascendancies and I would be a great guitarist. I would dethrone George Harrison. I bought a second hand guitar and took it with a Bert Weedon instruction book to my room. I nailed a message to the door saying 'DO NOT DISTURB UNTIL I AM A GREAT GUITARIST'. This was the first indication I'd ever had that my mother could read, she followed the instructions to the letter. I emerged a week later, an emaciated, skeletal figure with sore fingers and a total inability to even tune the bloody thing. After a few weeks' practice, however, I managed to string a few chords together. 'Great,' I thought, 'I'm on my way.' My father, though, had other ideas and took to clouting me round the ear and taking himself off to the pub whenever I picked it up. One terrible day I came in to find my musical aspirations in tatters alongside a demolished guitar. It had been trodden on. The old man maintained that it had been an accident but I had reason to doubt this as I used to keep it on top of the wardrobe. Thus my strumming career was consigned to the dustbin of broken dreams and all I had to show for weeks of putting my fingers through contortional hell was a busted guitar, a cauliflower ear and a parent with a drink problem. And George Harrison's position was safe.

I was never a great scholar, I was more interested in climbing the tree of life than carving my initials on the tree of knowledge and at fifteen I decided to leave. With a courage I never knew I had I marched into the principal's office and told him that I was going and that he couldn't stop me. He didn't try. So there I was fresh out of school and fresh out of work, but it wasn't for long. Through an old family friend I got a full time job in a betting office where I learned all the aspects of bookmaking, eventually becoming a settler and later a shop manager. It was during this period that I first took an interest in rhyming slang, picking up weird and wonderful phrases from both sides of the counter. I worked in shops all over London from the docklands – before dockers became an endangered species – to street market sites, to offices in the City. And my vocabulary blossomed.

At twenty-one my feet started to get itchy, there had to be more to life than 5-4 the field and the *Sporting Life* so I set out to find it. The next few years saw me drifting in and out of a variety of jobs, taking in snippets of slang wherever it could be found, from different tradesmen on a council building site in Hackney, from a saw doctor in a saw mill in Stratford and even an ex-pat Poplavian in a garage in Jersey.

In the early seventies whilst watching a dire sitcom on the television I just knew I could write a funny script. I now had a wife and a young son and this would make me rich. Move over Galton, Simpson, Speight and the rest, I was coming through. I wrote a comic master-piece called *Worms Up a Lamp Post* for which I received a bucketful of rejection slips. Philistines. Heads of television comedy departments wouldn't know a funny script if it crept up behind them and tickled them. Heeding the family motto, 'If at first you don't succeed pack it in', I watched sadly as another dream bit the dust.

In 1986 after nine years of driving a lorry for a London health authority I was made redundant. After a year of unemployment and a multitude of unanswered job applications I bought a small van and became a courier on a self employed basis. One day in 1989 a large northern driver of a large northern lorry tried to fit his vehicle into the back of mine. Whilst I was obeying a red traffic light he seized his opportunity but failed abysmally. All he managed to do was to write off my van and put me out of work for six months with an injured back.

It was during this spell of enforced idleness that the seeds of this book were planted. Unable to find a more up to date work than the one I possessed, which was first published in 1960, I came to the opinion that the world needed another.

This is it.

Acknowledgements

I would like to thank a few people for their help and encouragement in this project.

Firstly, my wife, Jean, for everything; my son Chris who didn't complain when I commandeered his word processor for six months; Amy and Larry Cook for their help in the early stages; Barry and the chaps at Lobword for the buckshee photocopying; Ron George for his contribution; Laura Morris for her advice; Lou for helping me when I needed it and the people of London who didn't know that there was somebody making a mental note of their words and wit.

Finally, thanks to Robson Books, especially Louise, Marcus and the troublemaker who answers the phone.

Abergavenny *Penny*
An old reference to an old penny which never made the transition into the world of decimals.

Ace of Spades *Aids*
An appropriate term, this being the traditional card of misfortune. A sufferer is said to have 'drawn the ace of spades'.

Ache & Pain *Rain*
Almost the norm for it to be 'aching' during Wimbledon fortnight or as England are about to win their only test of the series.

Acker Bilk *Milk*
A term formed in the 60s on the name of the West Country jazzman.

Adam & Eve *Believe*
Very old and very common and often an expression of disbelief, e.g., 'I can't Adam and Eve you said that.'

Adam Faith *Safe*
A term employed by betting shop managers in the 60s when Mr Faith was just an entertainer. Now that the man advises on financial matters it would appear to have more relevance. However, the large moneybox is still most commonly known as a 'Peter' and has been since the seventeenth century but nobody knows why.

Ain't She Sweet *Seat*
Normally reduced to an 'ain't she' it is what gentlemen gave to ladies on trains before it became sexist to do so.

Airs & Graces *1 Braces*
Quite common before this mode of support was supplanted by the belt.

2 Faces
Heard in a riverside pub not known for its salubrious clientele. 'Cor there's some dodgy looking airs in here tonight. Let's go somewhere else.'

Alan Minter *Splinter*
Used very briefly when the man was world middleweight boxing champion. It refers to a sliver of wood in the finger, hand or wherever.

Alan Whickers *Knickers*
TV inspired term based on the television personality.

Albert Hall *Wall*
Harassed parents may be driven up the Albert Hall by troublesome offspring.

All Behind *Blind*
Applies sympathetically to those who can't see but angrily to those who can but don't see, e.g., 'What do you mean you didn't see the red light, what are you all behind?'

All Complain *Rain*
This is one of the oldest terms in the book and one of the most appropriate. Wet weather brings out the moaner in all of us but on the plus side it does get the squeegee people away from traffic lights for a while.

Alligator *Later*
A 50s term formed on the title of the rock'n'roll record 'See You Later Alligator'.

Almond Rock *Cock*
The male member is well represented in the world of RS and several terms, like this one, take the form of a sweetmeat.

Almond Rock(s) *Sock(s)*
Very common and always condensed to 'almonds'.

Alphonse *Ponce*
Applies not only to a pimp but to a general sponger. An 'Alphonse' is someone who deliberately goes out with very little money and exploits the generosity or stupidity of his friends. Not a nice person!

Amos & Andy *Shandy*
A 50s term based on an American TV series of that time.

Amsterdam *Jam*
No matter what fruit it's made from it's all 'amster'.

Andy Cain *Rain*
An ancient piece that has disappeared down the drain.

Andy Capp *Tap (Borrow)*
Very fittingly based on a cartoon strip character who is forever skint and therefore always 'on the tap'.

Andy McNish *Fish*
Applies mainly to fish in its role as food.

Andy Pandy *Shandy*
Oft used term based on the TV puppet that everyone watched with mother but nobody admits to liking.

Anna Maria *Fire*
This applies to the domestic fire rather than anything a fireman would be interested in. The pronunciation of 'Maria' must rhyme with fire.

Anna May Wong *Pong*
Fairly old piece based on an actress of the silent screen.

Apple & Pip *Sip (Urinate)*
Uncommon example of a piece of RS for a term of back-slang. Sip is a back formation of piss, hence to 'go for an apple'.

Apple Cider *Spider*
The only hairy apple you'll ever see.

Apple Core   *Score*
A reference to £20.

Apple Fritter   *Bitter (Ale)*
The oldest of many terms for this kind of neck oil.

Apple Pie   *Sky*
It's a nice day when the 'currant's shining in the apple pie'.

Apple Pips   *Lips*
Who can resist nice rosy 'apples'.

Apple Tart   *Fart*
A disgusting stench often follows a dropped 'apple'.

Apples & Pears   *Stairs*
Probably the one term that everybody knows.

Apples & Rice   *Nice*
Generally shortened to the first element when describing something that *is* nice, e.g., 'She's apples'. But used in full when used to describe something that isn't, e.g., 'Oh that's very apples and rice. I'm out of work and you're pregnant again.'

Apple Sauce   *Horse*
One of the many terms for the noble steed although this may refer to the racehorse that came in last or 'ran like a pig'. Hence apple sauce.

April Fool(s)   *1 (Football) Pools*
Everybody's dream. To win the 'Aprils'.

2 Tool(s)
Originally referred to the tools of the burglary trade but later evolved to any tools of any trade.

3 Stool
A bar stool usually.

April Shower(s)   *Flower(s)*
A natural and quite common term. Can also refer to this brand of beer.

Aristotle   *Bottle*

Always reduced to 'Aris' it refers to any bottle and is also an instance of slang in reference to the backside. *See* BOTTLE & GLASS.

Arm & Leg

Egg

What a chocolate one will cost you at Easter.

Army & Navy

Gravy

An example that was first dished up in the field kitchens of World War One.

Artful Dodger

Lodger

This was an oft used term when it was common for householders to take in lodgers. Named after the Dickensian oppo of Oliver Twist.

Artful Fox

Box

An old theatrical expression regarding a box in that establishment.

Arthur Ashe

Cash

A contemporary piece coined by used car dealers and based on the name of a former Wimbledon tennis champion from the USA.

Arthur Bliss

Piss

Largely unheard of brother of MICKY (qv) that is used in the same way.

Ash & Oaks

Smokes (Cigarettes)

Commonly used when one smoker reminds others in his company that it is someone else's turn to hand the fags round, e.g., 'Who's turn is it to flash the ash?'

Auntie Ena

Cleaner

Refers to a lady 'what does' and appears in a rhyme.

Have you seen my Auntie Ena
In an office she's a cleaner
Met a bloke from Bethnal Greena
Since then Uncle hasn't seen 'er.

Auntie Lily

Silly

Generally truncated to the first element 'Don't be so auntie.'

Auntie Nellie *Belly*
An old and less used rival to DERBY KELLY (qv) and is mainly used to describe a belly ache, i.e., 'I've got a bit of trouble with my Auntie Nellie.'

Auntie Ruth *Tooth*
A person with a recently acquired gap in their dental collection may be asked 'Where's your Auntie Ruth gone?'

Aunt's Sisters *Ancestors*
A mildly amusing and relevant pun.

Autumn Leaf *Thief*
Close friends may be as thick as autumn leaves.

Ave Maria *Fire*
An infrequent rival of ANNA MARIA (qv).

Aylesbury Duck *Fuck*
Only employed in terms of not caring i.e. 'I couldn't give an Aylesbury.'

Ayrton Senna *Tenner (£10)*
An 'Ayrton' is a thoroughly modern piece based on the name of the Brazilian motor racing champion.

Baa Lamb *Tram*
Extinct term for an extinct mode (in London anyway) of transport. It is included because there has been talk about its making a comeback in an effort to combat London's traffic problems in the 90s. If it does, then RS is ready!

Babbling Brook *1 Cook*
In its original form a 'babbler' was an army cook of the first world war. It now applies to anyone who can wield a tin opener.

2 Crook
This is a later extension but is still reduced to 'babbler'.

Back Porch *Torch*
If there are no lights on your back porch then you'll need a 'back porch'.

Bacon & Egg(s) *Leg(s)*
Least popular of several expression for the original stocking fillers.

Baden Powell *Trowel*
An old term for the bricklayer's tool which is based on the name of the British general who founded the boy scout movement.

Bag of Flour *Shower*
A plain, old ablutionary term.

Baked Bean　　　***The Queen***
The old baked bean is a less than flattering term for Queen
Elizabeth II.

Baked Beans　　　***Jeans***
A terms that had to happen and did in the 60s with the rise
in popularity of both products. The cowboy connection
is also obvious.

Baked Potato　　　***Waiter***
One of several examples ending with 'potato' for the res-
taurant lackey.

Baker's Dozen　　　***Cousin***
An old term usually condensed to a 'bakers'.

Bald head　　　***Red***
Heard only in the snooker hall. Possibly from the saying
'as bald as a billiard ball'.

Ball & Bat　　　***Hat***
Although this is a very old term it has never achieved the
popularity of the ultra familiar TIT FOR TAT (qv).

Ball & Chain　　　***Strain***
Used sarcastically when a job is being done without much
effort, e.g., 'What, carrying one box at a time? Mind you
don't ball and chain yourself.' In non rhyming slang a ball
and chain is a spouse.

Ball of Chalk　　　***Walk***
Has famously stridden the road of RS for years.

Ball of Fat　　　***Cat***
Descriptive of many a pampered pussy.

Ball of Lead　　　***Head***
A piece first fired during World War One.

Balloon Car　　　***Saloon Bar***
Reduced to 'the balloon' this is one of the few terms to
effect a rhyme on both elements.

Balmy Breeze　　　***Cheese***
Any type, colour or texture. It's all 'balmy'.

Band of Hope **Soap**
A relevant piece based on an old organization that preached clean living to juveniles.

Barclays Bank **Wank (Masturbate)**
A fairly old piece for the 'flogging of the Horace'.

Barge & Tug **Mug**
Old rivermen would have had a 'barge of ROSIE LEE' (qv).

Bark & Growl **Trowel**
An archaic piece that's probably laid its last brick.

Barnaby Rudge **Judge**
A Dickens of a title for the legal bigwig.

Barnacle Bills **Pills (Testicles)**
A pill is an old slang term for a ball that has evolved quite happily to this extension and is responsible for 'tablets' and 'tabs', which also refer to man's dangly tender bits. The term is always reduced to 'barnacles'.

Barnet Fair **Hair**
Based on an event that dates back to medieval times, this old and very familiar term applies to a head of hair *en masse*. Or lack of mass when referring to a bald man who has 'got no Barnet'.

Barney Moke **Poke**
An old term for a wallet and its contents as used by a dip or skyman (pickpocket). This is also used as a reference to sexual intercourse.

Bar of Soap **1 Dope**
Used mainly in connection with drugs, although a dimwit can be a 'bar of soap'.

2 Pope
A disrespectful reference to his eminence, otherwise known a the holy SOAP & LATHER (qv).

3 Rope
An offer from a knight of the road to a broken down motorist, 'If you've got a bar of soap I'll give you a tow.'

Barry McGuigan **Big 'un**

Heard recently in a baker's shop. When asked which of the remaining three loaves he wanted a customer replied, 'the Barry McGuigan'. Ironic really because the man is a former world boxing champion at featherweight, which makes him a little 'un.

Basil Brush *Thrush*
A fungal infection, often of the genitals, that can be sexually transmitted. Based on the name of a television puppet.

Basin of Gravy *Baby*
A leaking, bawling, sleep reducing, time consuming, stress inducing, pocket emptying bundle of happiness. That's a 'basin'.

Bat & Ball *1 Stall*
From which wares may be sold.

2 Wall
Always used in full, as by the insomniac woman whose husband's snoring is 'driving me up the bat and ball'.

Bat & Wicket *Ticket*
Applies to any ticket from theatre to train including one for a test match.

Bath Bun *1 Son 2 Sun*
Not often used either way.

Battle Cruiser *Boozer*
Post-war term for the pub usually known as the 'battle'.

Battleship(s) *Lip(s)*
Refers to lips of the fuller variety and also to insolence. A child who answers his parents back may be told, 'We'll have a little less battle from you if you don't mind,' or more to the point, 'button your battle or you'll cop out'.

Bazaar *Bar*
When this term was coined it would have referred to an old 'spit and sawdust' bar. Were it being formed on the basis of a modern bar *Bizarre* would be more apt.

Bazooka *Snooker*

Modern example brought on by the popularity of snooker as a TV sport.

Beano & Dandy   *Shandy*
Another term for the beer and lemonade mixture. Based on the children's comics.

Bear's Paw   *Saw*
Hard to see why the paw of this particular animal should be used, a dog's would have been more obvious. Still it bears no scrutiny because this is a seldom heard term for the carpenter's tool.

Beattie & Babs   *Crabs (Crablice)*
Based on a music hall duo who probably deserved better.

Beechams Pill   *Bill*
In its modern form 'the beechams' applies to the police. Based on the name of the famous laxative the term appears particularly appropriate because just a glimpse of a police car in your rear view mirror can have exactly the same effect. Even when you've done nothing wrong. In its older form it refers to the advertising posters that appear on walls thus threatening the liberty of old Bill Stickers if he ever gets caught. Also a theatrical bill.

Beehive   *1 Dive*
Only used in connection with a footballer who 'takes a beehive' in the opposing penalty area in order to take an unfair advantage.

2 Five
Chiefly a bingo term that is sometimes heard in relation to £5.

Bees & Honey   *Money*
An old and once common term that has been taken over by 'bread'. *see* BREAD & HONEY.

In 1971, when the British currency was decimalized we not only lost some old friends but also some long established slang. These are some of them:

Ha'penny   *A Brown*
Penny   *Clod, Stiver, Coal, Yennep (Backslang)*

Threepenny Bit	*Daddler, Joey*
Sixpence	*Tanner, Kick, Sprazi*
One Shilling	*Deaner, Chip, Bob, Hog, Gen*
Eighteen Pence	*Kibosh*
Two Shillings	*Bice, Bice O' Deaners, Two Bob, Couple O'Bob, Flo, Two Ender*
Two and Sixpence	*Half a Crown, Tosheroon*
Five Shillings	*Dollar, Caser, Quarter, five bob*
Ten Shillings	*Ten Bob, Cows, Half, Net Gen*
One Pound	*Nicker, Quid, Stripe, Strike, Sov, Oncer, Bar, Sheet, Saucepan, Dunop (Backslang). By preceding each of these words with Half A we get more terms for Ten Shillings.*
Two Pounds	*Deuce, Bottle, Pair O'Nickers*
Three Pounds	*Carpet, Tray*
Four Pounds	*Rofe (Backslang)*
Five Pounds	*Jacks, Flim, Finn, Fiver, Revif (Backslang), Skydiver, Handful*
Six Pounds	*Exis (Backslang), Tom Mix, Sick Squid*
Seven Pounds	*Nevis (Backslang)*
Eight Pounds	*Garden*
Nine Pounds	*Feel, Mother, Scotsman*
Ten Pounds	*Tenner, Big 'Un, Cockle, Rennet (Backslang), Double Handful*
Twenty Pounds	*Score, Apple*
Twenty-Five Pounds	*Pony, Macaroni*
Fifty Pounds	*Half a Ton, Nifty, Bullseye*
One Hundred Pounds	*Ton, Century, One-Er*
Five Hundred Pounds	*Monkey*
One Thousand Pounds	*Grand, K, Long 'Un*
Two Thousand Pounds	*Archer*
	Other numbers in backslang: *1 Eno, 2 Owt, 3 Erth, 5 Evif, 8 Theg, 9 Enin, 10 Net.* *For pounds follow with Dunop, e.g. Owt Dunop = £2.*
Silver	*Snow, Tin, White, Revlis (Backslang)*
Gold	*Delog (Backslang)*
Copper	*Brown, Rust, Mouldies*
Small Change	*Tosh, Scratch*
	All terms from ten shillings (now 50p) are still in use.

Bee's Knees   *Business*
More of a pun than RS and refers to 'the business' meaning the best, the most excellent. The fact that it is so widely known rates inclusion.

Beeswax   *Tax*
Refers to Income Tax and is a clever cockney pun. Bees (money – *see* BEES & HONEY) whacks or 'money I've been whacked for', as a disgruntled worker may say on opening his paypacket.

Beetles & Ants   *Pants*
Applies to underpants and is reduced to 'beetles'.

Beezonker   *Shonker (nose)*
This is a nose of the large variety commonly associated with Jews. Originally a 'shonker' was a derogatory name for a Jew.

Beggar Boy's Arse   *Brass (Money)*
Always short changed to 'beggar boys' the phrase is ancient and apt. Brass is what the poor little sod would have been after and all he would have received is a kick up the backside.

Beggar my Neighbour   *Labour*
On the labour is another version of on the dole hence 'on the beggar' is to be out of work.

Beg your Pardon   *Garden*
Post-war term when people started to have gardens rather than back yards.

Belt & Braces   *Races*
A horse race meeting is the term's general employment.

Bended Knees   *Cheese*
Always sliced to a bit of 'bended'.

Benghazi   *Carzey (Lavatory)*
Always reduced to 'the Ben' the term probably emanated from World War Two. The battle for Benghazi was the allies' first major victory of the war. The word carzey or Khazi is an example of a slang that is based on the Italian language called Parlyaree. It was originally employed

by circus and fairground people but was adapted and popularized by mainstream theatricals especially in the BBC radio series 'Round the Horne'.

Ben Hur *Stir (Prison)*
A term coined after the success of the 1959 film.

Berkeley Hunt *Cunt*
An alternative to the next entry which has become infamous.

Berkshire Hunt *Cunt*
It is well documented that in its shortened form of 'Berk' the term has become accepted in all circles. It is never employed anatomically, a 'Berk' is a fool.

Bernhard Langer *Banger*
A contemporary term for a sausage, not necessarily a German one. Incidentally sausages and saveloys have long been known as 'bags of mystery' and more recently 'mystery bags'. Herr Langer is a champion golfer.

Beryl Reid *Lead (Dog's Leash)*
Probably greyhound track inspired. Named after the British comedienne.

Betty Grable *Table*
Called after a Hollywood actress noted for having a great pair of legs. Now she has two pairs.

Bessie Braddock *Haddock*
Based on the name of a British politician this mainly applies to the fish as a meal. Although there is no reason why one shouldn't go fishing for 'Bessies'.

Bexley Heath *Teeth*
One of several pieces rhyming Heath with chomping gear.

Big Bass Drum *Bum*
Reduced to 'big bass' obviously, this applies to a bottom of large proportions, or the one of a masochist that takes a beating.

Big Ben *Ten*

A reference to £10. Formerly ten shillings.

Big Ears **Cheers**
Used jocularly when raising a glass, formed on the name of the Enid Blyton character.

Big Ears & Noddy **Body**
Based on the names of Toytown's most prominent citizens it is spoken by the Chauvinist and dwarfed to 'Ere take a look at the Big Ears on this bird coming up the road.' The noise funnels won't come into it.

Bill & Ben **Pen**
Based on the names of the world's most famous flower pot men whom everybody thinks they can impersonate.

Bill O'Gorman **Foreman**
A term that dates back to the 19th century. Probably on a real life Irish ganger who couldn't possibly have known he would achieve immortality.

Bill Stickers **Knickers**
Said in the form of a name rather than an occupation.

Billy Bunter **1 Punter**
Mainly of betting shop usage and based on an old comic and TV character.

2 Shunter
Railwaymen's term.

Billy Button **Mutton**
19th century and now obsolete. Based on an old slang name for a tailor.

Billy Cotton **Rotten**
Formed on the name of an early television band leader this is what a disgruntled child called its father if he didn't come across with a tanner for an ice cream. Now the old man is called much worse if he doesn't weigh in with a week's wages for a pair of trainers.

Billy Smart **Fart**
When a pungent pong pervades the atmosphere, the words 'Bloody hell, who let Billy Smart in here?' are

usually followed by looks of disgust and probably one of nonchalance. Named after a circus proprietor.

Binnie Hale *Tale*
Oldish term for a conman's sob story that was in vogue when this actress was. But not any more.

Birch Broom *Room*
An ancient piece rarely, if ever, used nowadays. Refers to a room rather than room to manoeuvre.

Bird(s) & Bee(s) *Knee(s)*
An injured 'bird' is the mid leg crisis much dreaded by sporting folk.

Birdcage *Stage*
Where thespians put themselves on display.

Birdlime *Time*
Widely employed as 'bird' meaning a prison sentence.

Bird's Nest *1 Pest*
Chiefly relates to a child with a God given talent for driving adults mad.

2 Chest
A human chest especially a hairy one therefore presumably a male one. As opposed to MAE WEST (qv).

Biscuits & Cheese *Knees*
A term that is rare in that it cannot be used in the singular. Always broken down to 'biscuits'.

Bit & Piece *Niece*
Affectionately known by uncles as 'little bit', the prefix is important as it removes any aspect of distastefulness.

Bite(s) & Scratch(es) *Match(es)*
One of a number of terms for a box of lights.

Blackadder *Ladder*
New term inspired by the TV series of that name the star of which has climbed the 'blackadder' of success on the back of his creation.

Black & Blue *Cue*

The snooker or pool cue. Used as a club by the sound of it.

Black & White　　*1 Night*
Always used in full as to be woken in the middle of the 'black & white'.

2 Tight
A reference to meanness that is reduced to the first element whereby you may call a penny pincher a 'black' bastard without racist overtones.

Black Bess　　*Yes*
A definite affirmative is a 'big black bess'.

Blackbird & Thrush　　*Brush*
Chiefly applies to a shoe brush but may also take in a 'Hampstead' scrubber. *See* HAMPSTEAD HEATH.

Black Eye　　*Pie*
A term that was possibly born when somebody asked a barman for a SMACK IN THE EYE (qv).

Blackheath　　*Teeth*
Used in reference to those people who care not for dental cleanliness.

Blackman　　*Sister*
Kissed 'Er　　An old but obsolete term.

Black Maria　　*Fire*
Applies to a fire the emergency services would deal with, not a domestic one.

Blackpool Rock　　*Cock (Penis)*
This is one of many terms for the male member. Probably inspired by the song by George Formby.

Bladder of Lard　　*1 Card*
More especially a bingo card although it would have been a housey housey card on its formation.

2 Yard
'The Bladder' is a reference to New Scotland Yard.

Block of Ice　　*1 Dice*

Would appear to be one that is running cold.

2 Shice
Originally applied to unlicensed bookmakers at a race course. To shice is to 'do a runner' without paying out on winning wagers. Many a crooked bookie has had it 'over the wall', when his bag was full.

Blue & Grey　　*Day*
Probably an allusion to the colours of the sky.

Blue Moon　　*Spoon*
A term that dates back to the last century in respect of the utensil, without which eating soup would be a messy business.

Blue Peter　　*Heater*
Normally applies to the heat source in the car.

Board & Easel　　*Diesel*
An example that was first chalked up in the transport industry.

Boat Race　　*Face*
One of several terms for the 'mug' but now the commonest. Anyone with a dodgy boat is no oil painting.

Bob & Weave　　*Leave*
Time to 'bob & weave' or time we were 'bobbing & weaving'. Either way it's time to go.

Bob Hope　　*1 Soap*
Now the most familiar term for the lather cake. From the American comedian from South London.

2 Dope
A modern term relating to drugs.

Bob Squash　　*Wash*
An old term applicable to a public wash room. People using this facility hang up their jackets at their peril as it is a haven for pickpockets who are said to be 'working the Bob'.

Boiled Beef &　　*Claret*
Carrot
Nothing to do with wine. Shortened to the first two ele-

ments it refers to blood ie 'There was boiled beef all over the place.' Could describe the aftermath of a fight, an accident or the first day of the Harrods sale.

Boiled Sweet   *Seat*
Heard in the cafe 'You get the teas and I'll find some boiled sweets.'

Bolt the Door   *Whore*
From the lowest echelons of whoring came the 'old bolts', a corruption of which could be 'old boots' meaning ugly old hags. An ugly old term.

Bonny Dundee   *Flea*
An elderly term that used to be much more common than it is now.

Boo & Hiss   *Piss*
One of a multitude of examples for the act or urination. This particular term can also be used in the form of a send up, ie, 'taking the boo and hiss' and often serves for going on the booze.

Bootlace   *Case*
Mainly applies to a suitcase in which case to prevent a calamitous trip be sure to secure your 'bootlaces'.

Bo Peep   *Sleep*
Very common and often used with 'Little' as prefix.

Boracic Lint   *Skint*
Ultra familiar in reduced form of 'Brassic'. It is when we are in this state of financial incompetence that we find out who our friends are. (When boys have money they think they're men. But when they're brassic they're boys again.)

Borrow & Beg   *Egg*
An elderly example on the edge of extinction.

Bottle & Glass   *Arse*
This term not only serves anatomically but reduced to the first element is widely employed in relation to courage. Anyone who performs a brave or bold act is said to 'have a lot of bottle'. Wonder if the Milk Marketing

Board were aware of this when they bestowed upon us the benefits of their product during their famous advertising campaign. Whether they did or not I don't know, but they did put a piece of RS onto the tongues of a lot of people who were ignorant of the fact.

Bottle & Stopper   *Copper*
An old reference to a policeman.

Bottle of Beer   *Ear*
Always used in full, e.g., 'a word in your bottle of beer'. 'A word in your bottle' takes on an altogether different and unsavoury meaning. *See* BOTTLE & GLASS.

Bottle of Booze   *News*
A fairly recent example that chiefly refers to the news on television, e.g. 'Turn the telly on I want to see the bottle of booze.'

Bottles of Booze   *Shoes*
One of a number of terms for the 'plate holders'.

Bottle of Fizz   *Whizz*
Whizzing is stealing quickly as the opportunity arises. Often for a pickpocket.

Bottle of Pop   *Wop (Italian)*
Known as a 'bottler' which in itself means a coward or one who lacks 'bottle'. *See* BOTTLE & GLASS. This is the typical generalization of the Italian soldier of World War Two.

Bottle of Sauce   *Horse*
Refers to one that pulls a cart rather than a racehorse.

Bottle of Scotch   *Watch*
On its formation this referred to a pocket watch. It is that old.

Bottle of Spruce   *Deuce*
In its original form this applied to two pence but is now more readily associated with £2. It also applies to the playing card and odds of 2/1 are also known as 'bottle'. Formed on the name of a cheap and nasty concoction known as spruce beer. Incidentally, deuce is another in-

stance of parlyaree. *See* BENGHAZI for explanation.

Bottle Top *Cop*
This has nothing to do with the police but to value. Anything that is 'not much bottle' is worthless.

Bow & Arrow *Sparrow*
A bird much in the affection of Londoners.

Bow & Quiver *Liver*
Refers to the organ and offal but mainly to feeling liverish or irritable.

Bowler Hat *Rat*
The rodent or an untrustworthy person.

Box of Toys *Noise*
A vociferous person will be told to 'hold your box of toys.'

Box of Tricks *Flicks*
The flicks is old slang for the cinema and when this term was coined it would have been very apt.

Boy Scout *Shout*
An appropriate term in that these young bob-a-jobbers do a lot of shouting around the camp fire. Well they call it singing but did you ever see the Gang Show?

Boy(s) & Girl(s) *Twirl(s)*
An underworld term for a skeleton key.

Boys in Blue *Stew*
Nothing to do with food but to be in a 'right old boys in blue' is to be in a state of agitation.

Brace & bits *Tits*
Not widely used but when it is it is reduced to 'braces'.

Brahms & Liszt *Pissed*
A theatrical term that enjoys wide usage. A variant of MOZART & LISZT (qv).

Brands Hatch *Scratch*
In all its forms from relieving an itch to the slight injury or

telling someone to get lost, 'Go scratch yourself' becomes 'Go Brands Hatch'.

Brass Band(s) *Hand(s)*
One of several terms of reference for the forks.

Brass Monkey *Dunkie (Condom)*
So called because it offers no protection from frost. So be careful when making love in the open on a cold night.

Brass Nail *Tail (Prostitute)*
Reduced to 'brass' this is very familiar. To dress gaudily as this lady may do, is to appear 'brassy'.

Brass Tacks *Facts*
A piece of RS that has gone up in the world.

Brave & Bold *Cold*
A rival to 'TATERS IN THE MOULD' (qv) on the cold front. Does not apply to being unwell.

Bread & Butter *1 Gutter*
Very old example when used in relation to being down and out or 'in the bread and butter'.

2 Nutter
A newer adaptation when referring to anyone that is a stump short of a wicket.

3 Putter
A television golf commentator's term.

Bread & Cheese *Sneeze*
Used complete, e.g., 'an attack of the bread and cheeses'.

Bread & Honey *Money*
Shortened to 'bread' its fame is universal.

Bread & Jam *1 Tram*
An old term that was made redundant with the disappearance of this mode of transport.

Bread & Lard *Hard*
Used sarcastically to anyone complaining unnecessarily, e.g., 'So your dishwasher is broken is it? Well how bloody

bread and lard for you.'

Breadcrumbs   *Gums*
A piece of graffiti seen on a lorry, 'Linda Lovelace's dentist reckons she's got the finest breadcrumbs he's ever come across.'

Brewer's Bung   *Tongue*
A fairly common example for what is also known as the red rag.

Brian O'Linn   *Gin*
A very old term and one of many for this particular drink.

Bricks & Mortar   *Daughter*
An old term that has fallen into disuse.

Bride & Groom   *1 Broom*
A new 'bride' sweeps clean.

2 Room
A room or space to manoeuvre.

Bright & Frisky   *Whisky*
The term seems to be based on the result of a few but not too many. Sometimes called a 'Brighton'.

Brighton Pier   *Queer*
A 'Brighton' is a homosexual.

Brighton Rock   *Cock (Penis)*
Another of numerous terms linking this part of the anatomy and the seaside sweet.

Brig's Rest   *Vest*
A rough itchy undergarment once given to convicts.

Bristol City   *Titty*
Very common when reduced to 'Bristols'.

British Rail   *Stale*
An obvious allusion to the infamous inter-city sandwich.

Brother Bung *Tongue*
Reduced to the first element and often used as a warning as, 'That brother of yours will get you into trouble one of these days.' The term, which was used as a brand name for a pickle company, is based on old slang for a brewer, who was known as a 'Brother of the Bung'. Other examples in the same vein were 'Brother of the Blade' (soldier), 'Brother of the String' (fiddler) and 'Brother of the Gusset' (pimp).

Brown & Mild *Wild*
Refers to the loss of temper and based on two types of beer that are often mixed.

Brown Bess *Yes*
An ancient variant of BLACK BESS (qv) based on the name given to a flintlock rifle.

Brown Bread *Dead*
Old and most common term for the popping of the clogs.

Brown Hat *Cat*
An old term for old Felix.

Brown Joe *No*
The equally aged partner of BROWN BESS (qv).

Brown Paper *Caper (Game)*
Asked of anyone doing something he shouldn't be doing in a place he shouldn't be doing it, 'What's your brown paper then?'

Brussels Sprout *1 (Boy) Scout*
A term almost as old as the movement.

2 Tout
Originally used on the racecourse concerning the professional tipsters. Now in general use for anyone who sells tickets at highly exorbitant rates.

Bryant & Mays *Stays*
An outmoded piece for an unfashionable garment. Based on the well known matchstick men.

Bubble & Blister *Sister*
Closely related to SKIN & BLISTER (qv) but not as common.

Bubble & Squeak *1 Beak (magistrate)*
Known as being 'up before the bubble'. Named after a dish made up of fried leftovers.

2 Greek
Very familiar in shortened form of 'bubble'.

3 Speak
To 'put the bubble in' is to inform or to say something to cause trouble.

4 Weak
A sick person may come over all 'bubble and squeak'.

5 Week
Seven days is a 'bubble'.

Buck & Doe *Snow*
Normally said with heavy emphasis to create an illusion of an expletive, e.g., 'Look at the buck'n'doe out there.'

Bucket Afloat *Coat*
An old term with nautical connections. A bucket is an old term for a ship. World War One soldiers changed it to bucket and float.

Bucket & Pail *Jail*
For a shorter sentence say, 'in the bucket'.

Bucket & Spade *Maid*
In normal terms of reference a bar maid.

Bucket & Well *Hell*
Said in full to replace the F word, e.g., 'What the bucket and well was all that about?' could be asked of a girl, who on a first date takes you to see a film by Fellini.

Buckle My Shoe *Jew*
Old but now largely unheard of term.

Buckshee *Free*
Funny how this kind of beer always tastes better.

Bucks Hussar

Cigar
An example that seems to have been stubbed out.

Buddy Holly

1 Volley
Based on the late lamented rock singer this is a TV football commentator's term for kicking a ball before it bounces.

2 Wally
A pickled cucumber sold in the fish'n'chip shop has long been known as a 'wally'. Now it is sometimes known as a 'Buddy'. A Texan born in 1936, he was killed in a plane crash in 1959.

Bug & Flea

Tea
An unappetizing piece for a cuppa.

Bugs Bunny

Money
Fairly modern term based on the cartoon rabbit and short changed to 'Bugs' or 'Bugsy'. In backslang money becomes 'Yenom'.

Bull & Bush

Push
Generally preceded by 'the old' it refers to being dismissed from a job. Based on the music hall song extolling the virtues of the pub in Hampstead NW London.

Bull & Cow

Row
An altercation often between man and wife. Many a bar stool is occupied every night because of a 'bull and cow' with 'the trouble'. *See* TROUBLE AND STRIFE.

Bulldozer

Poseur
A contemporary piece for those annoying people who go to the 'right' places just to be seen.

Bullock's Horn

Pawn
An archaic term that is always reduced to the first element. Pertaining to a pledge made at 'uncles.'

Bullock's Liver

River
An example that got the chop years ago.

Bully Beef

Chief
Old reference to a prison warder.

Bung It In *Gin*
A not too common term for the all too common drink.

Burke & Hare *Chair*
Based on the names of the infamous 19th century body snatchers this is one of many terms for the piece of furniture.

Burn & Smoulder *Shoulder*
Apt when you've done the mad dogs and Englishmen bit and have incurred shoulders that could stop traffic.

Burnt Cinder *Window*
Always cut down to 'burnt'. Smash and grab merchants would 'sling the brick through the burnt, grab the loot and scarper'.

Burton on Trent *Rent*
May be no coincidence that the name of this famous brewery town should be used when very often the rent money was spent on its product.

Bushel & Peck *Neck*
An old term that often applies to the inside of the neck as well as the out. On a cold day one may be handed a hot cup of tea with the advice, 'Get that down your bushel and warm your cockles.'

Bushel of Coke *Bloke*
An ancient term now burnt out.

Bushy Park *Lark*
Refers to messing about. Formed on the name of the park by Hampton Court.

Butcher's Hook *Look*
Widely used and always reduced to the first element.

Buttercup & Daisy *Crazy*
Localized term used by a distraught father, e.g., 'Those kids are driving me buttercup.'

Butter Churn *Turn*
A theatrical term for a theatrical act.

Butterfly   *Tie*
An alternative to the very common PECKHAM RYE (qv) but is more descriptive of and may relate more easily to a bow-tie.

Buttons & Bows   *Toes*
'Shall we have it on our buttons?' is an invitation to leave.

By Pass   *Arse*
A good kick up the 'by pass' may be just what's needed to get a layabout going.

Cabin Cruiser   *Boozer*
Sometimes used as a variation of BATTLE CRUISER (qv).

Cain & Abel   *Table*
Oft used example based on the biblical brothers.

Callard & Bowsers   *Trousers*
Named after the well known confectioners and normally
taken down to 'Callards'.

Camden Town   *Brown*
A brown is an old slang term for a copper coin.

Cameroon   *Coon*
A term which came into being after the 1990 World Cup
when the team of that country performed so well.

Canary   *Fairy*
A reference to a homosexual male, a group of whom are
known as a 'bunch of canaries'.

Canal Boat   *Tote*
A piece from the racecourse for the totalisator.

Candle & Sconce   *Ponce*
Applies mainly to a pimp but a 'candle' is sometimes used
in the same way as ALPHONSE (qv).

Canoe(s)   *Shoe(s)*
As worn by people whose visible means of support are on

the larger side.

Can of Oil   *Boil*
Refers to the great pus filled swelling on the skin and normally reduced to a 'canov'.

Cape Horn   *Corn*
A reference to that shoe full of misery.

Cape of Good Hope *Soap*
Probably the nautical variation on a clean theme.

Capital City   *Tittie*
Contracted to 'capitals' normally in relation to those of ample proportions.

Captain Cook   *Book*
Originally applied to any book but was later adopted by the racing fraternity to include the book made at the track. Inspired by the British explorer (1728–79).

Captain Kirk   *Work*
Based on the boldly venturing hero of television's *Star Trek* which probably has a connection with the fact that during the recession of early 1990s, when the term was coined, people had more chance of flying to the moon than finding work.

Captain Morgan   *Organ*
Applies to any organ musical or otherwise. Formed on the name of the Welsh pirate (1635–88) who instead of being executed for his crimes was knighted and sent to govern Jamaica. Who says crime doesn't pay?

Captain Scott   *Hot*
Typical East End humour to use the name of a man who froze to death as a term pertaining to heat. Captain Robert Falcon Scott (b. 1868) died on an expedition to the South Pole in 1912.

Carbuncle   *Uncle*
The dictionary describes a carbuncle thus: 'An extensive skin eruption resembling a boil but much larger and having many openings.' Would appear to sum up an uncle quite nicely.

Cardboard Box   *Pox*
A recent formation and one of many for the disease you wouldn't tell your mother about.

Careless Talk   *Chalk*
Post-war term employed mainly by darts players.

Carl Rosa   *Poseur*
This alternative to BULLDOZER (qv) is based on a defunct operatic society.

Car Park   *Nark*
Possibly coined because an empty car park would provide the desired secrecy between the police and an informant 'nark'.

Carpet Bag   *Drag*
In its original form a 'carpet' is a three month prison sentence. It has now passed into a common term for the number three. Odds of 3/1 is a carpet as is £3.

Carving Knife   *Wife*
She of the sharp tongue and the cutting glances is known as 'the carving'.

Casablanca   *Wanker*
Mainly used in full but sometimes reduced to 'cazza' it is one of several terms for an unlikeable person.

Cash & Carry   *Marry*
This begets two offspring:
CASH & CARRIED, CASH & CARRIAGE.

Caster Oil(s)   *Royal(s)*
This 'casters' is a disrespectful name given to the royal family.

Caster & Pollux   *Bollocks*
The names of the twins of Gemini are transferred to the twins of the ball bag.

Castle Rag   *Flag*
This is one of the oldest pieces of RS because in its original form it applied to a four penny piece otherwise known as a groat. The slang for this coin was a flag. The

31

term now applies quite suitably to that which is flown.

Cat & Dog   *Bog*
The bog being a vulgar term for the lavatory.

Cat & Mouse   *House*
When this piece was coined many houses had both.

Cattle Truck   *Fuck*
Common in most forms of the word and always reduced to the first element. It is mainly used as 'cattled' meaning tired or rendered helpless (having two flat tyres for instance). It is also a suggestion as to what a source of irritation may do to himself, e.g., 'Get Cattled'. And it is what British tennis players usually get in the first round at Wimbledon. 'Cattle' or 'cattling' may be used with a sexual connotation.

Cellar Flap   *Tap*
One applied to tap dancing but now means to borrow.

Chain & Crank   *Bank*
An obsolescent piece that never created much interest.

Chain & Locket   *Pocket*
An uncommon rival to the ever popular SKY ROCKET (qv).

Chalfont St Giles   *Piles*
The 'chalfonts' is a theatrical term for haemorrhoids.

Chalk Farm(s)   *1 Arm(s)*
An ancient piece widely known as 'chalks'.

2 Harm
Of secondary usage.

Chalky White   *Light (Ale)*
'A chalky' is one of several terms for this beer.

Charing Cross   *Horse*
In old cockney dialect 'cross' was pronounced 'crorse' but horses are still known as 'Charings'.

Charlie Brown   *Clown*
A professional jester or anyone who acts the fool. From a

song of the 1950s.

Charlie Chan　　*Can*
Started with an advertising campaign for canned beer in the 1970s. From the fictional Chinese detective.

Charlie Dicken　　*Chicken*
The name of the great author is suggested here, albeit incorrectly, but RS isn't that particular. It refers to poultry, not cowardice.

Charlie Dilke　　*Milk*
Very old term that may have referred to the milkman as well as the product.

Charlie Howard　　*Coward*
Possibly responsible for the well known term of cowardice, 'to turn Charlie'.

Charlie Hunt　　*Cunt*
Widely used in respectable circles but only in respect of a fool, nothing stronger, e.g., 'I felt a right Charlie, I told everyone this dog would win and it came last.'

Charlie Mason　　*Basin*
The most common usage of this is as an expression of willingness to try something, e.g., 'I'll have a basin full of that.'

Charlie Pope　　*Soap*
A piece coined by the soldiers of the Great War.

Charlie Prescott　　*Waistcoat*
An old term for that part of a 'three piece whistle' which is pronounced 'westcot'.

Charlie Randy　　*Brandy*
Extremely old and probably obsolete term.

Charlie Ronce　　*Ponce*
The brother of JOE (qv). Must be the family line. Always shortened to 'Charlie'.

Charlie Smirke　　*Berk*
Formed on the name of an ex-jockey and used as an ex-

ample of secondary RS (*See* BERKSHIRE HUNT). Must be used in full because of the presence of CHARLIE HUNT (qv).

Charlie Wiggins

Diggins
A theatrical term for lodgings.

Charlton & Greenwich

Spinach
A greengrocer's term for Popeye's favourite.

Charming Wife

Knife
Early military term. She may have been introduced to German soldiers c.1914–18.

Chas & Dave

Shave
A modern term that is ironic in as much as the trademarks of these two cockney entertainers are their beards.

Chatham & Dover

Over
A piece taken from the Old London, Chatham and Dover railway line and used to emphasize finality, i.e., 'That's it, finished, all Chatham and Dover.'

Cherry Hog

Dog
Widely used term that relates to all mutts especially greyhounds. To go dog racing is to go to 'the cherries'. A cherry hog, by the way, is the stone of that fruit. In the early days of this century children would use them as playthings. Tell that to children of today and they'd zap you with their video game control unit.

Cherry Ripe

1 Pipe
Refers to that which is smoked.

2 Tripe
Written or spoken nonsense, e.g., 'What a load of cherry.'

Chevy Chase

Face
This has nothing to do with the American comedian of that name. This is actually one of the earliest examples of RS and refers to an ancient ballad about the battle of Otterburn which arose from a hunt near the Cheviot Hills in 1388.

Chicken Hearted

Farted

Used when the fetid fragrance of a faecal nature assails the nostrils, e.g., 'Who's chicken hearted?'

Chicken Perch *Church*
Known as the 'chicken' as all cockney parsons know.

Chimney & Soot *Foot*
The sock filler not the measurement.

China Plate *Mate*
The archetypical greeting from one cockney to another is 'Wotcher me ol' china'. But it has to be said that it is heard more often coming from a 'Hollywood' cockney than a real one. The term is, however, still in use often talking about 'a china of mine'.

Choc Ice *Dice*
Refer to those that come with games rather than gambling dice.

Chocolate Eclair *Prayer*
Kiddies say their 'chocolates' at bed time.

Chocolate Frog *Wog*
A piece that has arrived here from Australia via Earls Court.

Chocolate Fudge *Judge*
Said of a judge who has shown leniency 'I though I'd go down but the Chocolate let me off with a suspended.'

Chop sticks *Six*
A bingo term.

Christmas Card(s) *Guard(s)*
Takes in all types including a lookout, a railway guard and the soldiers that mind the Queen's gaff.

Christmas Cheer *Beer*
A drunk may be able to state in all honesty, 'The last time I was sober was eight Christmases ago.'

Christmas Crackers *Knackers (Testicles)*
The pulling of which is guaranteed to make the eyes water. Also used in terms of being exhausted, e.g.,

'Christmas crackered'.

Christmas Dinner   *Winner*
As contained in the late editions of evening newspapers referring to the racing results.

Christmas Eve   *Believe*
A rare alternative to ADAM & EVE (qv).

Christmas Log   *Dog*
A reference to greyhound racing.

Christmas Shop(ping)   *Strop(ping) (Masturbation)*
Doing your Christmas shopping in the privacy of your own home doesn't necessarily mean you have the Argos catalogue.

Cilla Black   *Back*
A 'dodgy Cilla' is a television script writer's term for a bad back. Based on the singer whose voice gives a lot of people a bad head. Not me though, Cilla. Not me.

Cinderella   *1 Smeller (Nose)*
Another of the many terms concerning the proboscis.

Yellow
Can be anyone who lacks moral fibre. Also a snooker ball.

Clark Gable   *Table*
A fairly recent rival of CAIN & ABEL (qv), based on the US film star who was known as the King of Hollywood (1901–60).

Clever Dick   *Brick*
A modern variant of KING DICK (qv).

Clever Dickie   *Brickie*
He who lays the clever dicks.

Clever Mike   *Bike*
More relevant today than when the term was formed due to the stunts performed on modern bicycles.

Clod Hopper   *Copper*

This is an old reference to copper coinage, namely a penny which was universally known as a 'clod'.

Clothes Peg(s)   *Leg(s)*
One of many terms for the personal supporters.

Cloud Seven   *Heaven*
Very common expression of happiness.

Coachman on the Box   *Pox*
Obviously a very old term for VD and shortened to 'the coachmans'.

Coal(s) & Coke   *Broke*
Refers to being potless. Or more specifically devoid of the pot that is required to urinate in.

Coal Heaver   *Stever*
An obsolete example for an old slang term for a penny.

Coalman's Sack   *Black*
Instruction from parent to grubby child at bed time. 'Go and have a wash, you're like the coalman's sack.' Therefore, the term only applies to being dirty.

Coat & Badge   *Cadge*
Formed on the name of the Doggett's coat and badge which is the oldest annual sporting event in Britain. Contested by rowers, the course is the 4½ miles stretch of the Thames between London Bridge and Cadogan Pier, Chelsea. The term is normally used in full but people on the tap are often said to be 'on the doggetts'.

Coat Hanger   *Banger*
Mainly refers to an old car but sometimes to a sausage.

Cobbler's Awls   *Balls*
The most common of all the terms for the testicles. Always reduced to 'cobblers'.

Cobbler's Stalls   *Balls*
Another version of the above.

Cob of Coal   *Dole*
One of the older examples for Unemployment Benefit.

Cock & Hen

1 Pen
Oldest of the terms for a scribbler.

2 Ten
A shortening of COCKEREL & HEN (qv).

Cocked Hat

Rat
Doesn't apply to the rodent but to a littleworth, i.e. someone not to be trusted or an informer.

Cockerel & Hen

Ten
Always reduced to a 'cockle', which is a lazy pronunciation of the first element, this originally applied to ten shillings but has survived decimalization and has been revalued to boot. It is now £10. 'A cockle' is also a ten year prison sentence.

Cock Linnet

Minute
Lends itself to the amount of time one will be away even if it will be longer, e.g., 'Won't be a cock linnet, I've just got to put on my boots.'

Cockroach

Coach
Refers to that vehicle that goes too fast on the motorway.

Cock Sparrow

Barrow
Commonly used by market traders.

Coffee & Cocoa

Say So
Common but unusual in that it is always reduced to the second element either as a term of disbelief, e.g., ' Do you think he'd be selling a car that cheap if there wasn't something wrong with it? I should cocoa!', or as one of factual emphasis, 'Has he made a fortune out of selling monkey cars to mugs like you? I should cocoa.'

Coffee & Tea

Sea
Nice to get away and dip your feet in the 'coffee' but you have to be careful these days, what with the dumping of waste and sewage, oil tanker accidents and the crimes of Saddam Hussein many of the world's seas are murkier than these beverages.

Coffee Stalls

Balls

Shrunk to the 'coffees' this is another term concerning men's nether regions.

Cold Potato *Waiter*
Normally refers to a slow one as opposed to HOT POTATO (qv).

Coldstream Guards *Cards*
Applies to playing cards.

Collar & Tie *1 Spy*
Usually refers to somebody at work who runs bosswards with tales of everyday shirking folk.

2 Lie
Old term that has been overtaken by PORK PIE (qv).

Collar & Cuff *Puff*
An old term for a homosexual.

Colleen Bawn *Horn (Erection)*
At a stroke this is reduced to having 'a colly on' and is based on the name of a 19th century operatic character.

Colney Hatch *Match*
Based on the name of a famous mental institution in North London in regard to what some mental patients shouldn't play with.

Colonel Blimp *Shrimp*
Applies only to the seafood.

Colonel Prescott *Waistcoat*
Apparently based on a sporting gentleman whose game, mayhap, was snooker.

Comb & Brush *Lush*
An elderly term for an alcoholic which originally stood for the demon drink itself.

Come & Go *Snow*
Vulgarists enjoy reducing this to the first element, e.g., 'There's no racing at Sandown 'cos there's come on the course.' In the extended form of COMING & GOING for snowing the same uncouth yob may state that, 'Someone up

there is coming all over the place.'

Come a Tumble   *Rumble.*
That is rumble in the sense of finding or being found out.
A worker who regularly ventures into the black economy
may be told, 'If your boss comes a tumble he'll march you
straight down the nick.' Alternatively he may be told 'If
you don't use your brains you'll come a tumble.' A very
appropriate term in that it signifies a downfall.

Comic Cuts   *Nuts*
Nuts is one of several euphemisms for the testicles. This
term is always reduced to 'comics'.

Conan Doyle   *Boil*
Based on Sir Arthur Conan Doyle (1859–1930), the
author who gave us Sherlock Holmes, this applies to the
large septic beast that appears on the skin. Always known
as a 'Conan'.

Constant Screecher   *Teacher*
Relevant more to teachers of yesteryear than today's who
seem more likely to be screeched at.

Constipation   *Station*
A probable allusion to motionless trains.

Corned Beef   *Thief*
A fairly modern piece that hasn't supplanted the
evergreen TEA LEAF (qv).

Corn(s) and   *Onion(s)*
Bunion(s)
A greengrocery term that also implies great skill, wisdom,
knowledge or street credibility, e.g., 'He knew his corns
and bunions when it came to painting.' A cockney sum-
mation of Michelangelo.

Corn Flake   *Fake*
Anything that isn't what it seems including funny money,
snide jewellery and that 300 year old chair that was made
last week.

Cornish Pasty   *Tasty*
Generally used in relation to the opposite sex and
chewed down to the first element, e.g., 'She's a bit

Cornish.'

Cough & Drag   *Fag*
Very suitable term for a cigarette and used in the context of going for a smoke. On his way to the toilet a worker may ask a colleague to 'cover for me while I nip out for a cough and drag'.

Cough & Sneeze   *Cheese*
Chiefly a grocer's term. Not to be confused with:

Cough & Splutter   *Butter*
If this comes from the same grocers as the previous item it's a good place not to do your shopping.

Council Houses   *Trousers*
A fairly modern reference to leg holders.

Country Cousin   *Dozen*
Mainly a phrase of the turf.

Couple O' Bob   *1 Gob (phlegm)*
If you see a couple of bob lying in the road it's more likely to be a green Gilbert than money.

                 2 Job
An unemployed person's desire is to go out and find a 'couple of bob'. A bob is a predecimalization word for 5 pence.

                 3 Swab
In its oldest form the term applies to a damp rag much sought after by pub darts players.

Cousin Ella   *Umbrella*
Probably the only cousin you've got that's in any way useful.

Covent Garden   *Pardon*
Can be begged and granted. Originally applied to a farthing, a long extinct coin.

Covered Wagon   *Dragon*
Applies to an ugly or disagreeable woman.

Cow & Calf   *Laugh*

Old term and used as, 'We had a right cow and calf down the Bull last night.' The victim of a mishap may ask a smirking spectator, 'What are you cowing at?'

Cow's Calf   *Half*
Refers to 50 pence or half a quid. Was originally 'cow and calf' but is now used extensively as a 'cows.'

Cow's Lick   *Nick*
An insider's reference to prison.

Cream Cracker(s)   *Knacker(s)*
The main employment for this is in connection with being exhausted, i.e., 'All that walking has left me cream crackered.'

Cribbage Peg   *Leg*
One of several terms linking leg with peg making them the most closely associated partners in rhyme.

Crimea   *Beer*
Formed by soldiers of a bygone century. The Light (Ale) Brigade perhaps.

Crocodile   *Smile*
Said to someone who looks down 'Come on, give us a crocodile.'

Crowded Space   *(Suit) Case*
A term used by thieves who made a living stealing luggage from railway stations and other crowded spaces.

Crown & Anchor   *Wanker*
Another term for someone who does not meet with approval.

Crown Jewels   *Tools*
Appropriate since a tradesman's tools are precious to him. A sometimes reference to a man's baby making equipment especially the main member.

Crust of Bread   *Head*
Applies anatomically rather than mentally. You don't use your crust but it may be scratched.

Cucumber	***Number***

Cucumber   ***Number***
Mainly used in connection with a telephone number, e.g., 'Give me your cucumber and I'll ring you back.'

Cuddle & Kiss   ***Piss***
Quite common when slashed to the first element. e.g., 'Watch my beer I'm just going for a cuddle.' Sometimes employed in its entirety as an alternative to MICKY BLISS (qv). Whereby a liberty taker, like a West End ice cream seller may be told to 'poke his overpriced cornet up his gonga because he is taking the cuddle and kiss.'

Cup of Tea   ***1 Pee/Wee***
If you hear somebody in the pub announce that he is going for a 'cup of tea' he isn't.

2 See
Used mainly as a term of farewell, e.g., 'I'll cup of tea you later.'

Currant Bun   ***1 Run***
More specifically on the run. Rivalling HOT CROSS BUN (qv).

2 Son
Father's little 'currant.'

3 Sun
Very familiar term known as 'the Currant'. Also used for the *Sun* newspaper.

Currant Cakes   ***Shakes***
Refers to having the DTs (Delirium Tremens).

Currant Cakie   ***Shaky***
Descriptive of how one may feel following a drunken spree or any circumstance that would make one feel wobbly.

Currants & Plums   ***Gums***
An invitation to a toothless person to smile is 'Come on, flash your currants.'

Custard & Jelly   ***Telly***
Most common excuse for going out is 'Well there's nothing on the custard.'

Custard Cream **Dream**
Bo Peep perchance to custard, as Shakespeare may have written had he come from Stratford E15.

Cut & Carried **Married**
A term of unavailability usually of a married woman.

Cut(s) & **Match(es)**
Scratch(es) An old but still burning reference to 'strikes'.

Cyril Lord **Bald**
Suitable since this is based on the name of a carpet and rug manufacturer and rug is a slang word for a wig.

Dad & Mum   *Rum*
Often referred to as a tot of 'daddy'.

Dad's Army   *Barmy*
A modernish term named after the TV series that is applied to someone who may be a penny short of a shilling, e.g., 'I don't trust him, he looks a bit dad's army to me.'

Daffadown Dilly   *Silly*
Always condensed to 'daffy' in reference to a scatter brain. Based on the ancient expression daffy-down-dilly meaning a dandy.

Daft & Barmy   *Army*
a modern equivalent of the old trouper KATE KARNEY (qv).

Daily Express   *Dress*
Refers to the garment and the act of getting dressed, which we do daily and swiftly on cold mornings.

Daily Mail   *1 Ale*
Going for a pint of 'daily' is a reference to going to the pub.

2 Nail
Mainly employed in the carpentry trade.

3 Tail
This takes in tail in many guises. It's the backside whereby a busy man may 'work his tail off'. It also means to follow

45

when it is common for a PC to be on a suspect's 'daily'. It's the prostitute more commonly associated with BRASS NAIL (qv) and the waggable part of a dog.

4 Tale
As told by a conman or a sneaky snitcher.

Dairy Box　　*Pox*
Formed on the name of a popular chocolate assortment and reduced to 'the dairy' it refers to venereal disease.

Daisy Bell　　*Hell*
Expressions of anger, disappointment or frustration are 'blooming', 'bloody', or 'fucking daisy' formed on the name of a music hall song title.

Daisy Dormer　　*Warmer*
Based on the name of a music hall artiste this ancient term probably originally referred to a bed warmer. It also describes springtime weather.

Daisy Roots　　*Boots*
Famous old term for trottercases.

Damn & Blast　　*Last*
Heard at a racecourse, 'Damn and blast, my horse came in damn and blast.'

Dan Leno　　*Beano*
Formed on the name of a famed music hall comedian, a beano is an outing to the seaside in a 'chara'. Dan Leno (1860–1904) was the first superstar of British comedy.

Danny La Rue　　*Blue*
Based on the well known entertainer this applies to anything blue including a joke, a film, snooker ball, etc.

Darby & Joan　　*1 Alone*
A loner spends most of his time on his Darby.

2 Phone
Least used of several terms for the telephone.

3 Moan
Based on an elderly married couple of an 18th century ballad this would appear to be a pertinent term since one

of the favourite pastimes of old people is moaning.

Darby Bands   *Hands*
Derived from an ancient phrase 'Father Darby's bands' which was a binding agreement between a money lender and a debtor which was heavily stacked on the lender's side. Such was the restrictive burden on the debtor that Darbies is a slang term for handcuffs.

Darling Buds of May *Gay (Homosexual)*
Proof of the ever widening glossary of RS, this TV series was on in the spring of '91 and by the summer a gay barman was nicknamed 'Darling Buds'.

Darling Daughter   *Water*
One of a numerous array of examples for what a fish goes about his business in.

Darling Wife   *Knife*
A variation of CHARMING WIFE (qv).

David Bowie   *Blowy (Windy)*
Spoken with great cockney understatement after the great hurricane of 1987 that devastated the south of England. 'A bit David Bowie last night wasn't it!' It was like saying the Pope is a bit religious.

Davy Crockett   *Pocket*
A 50s term based on the name of the early American frontiersman and politician who was born in 1786 and killed at the battle of the Alamo in 1836.

Davy Jones's Locker   *Knocker*
Refers to a door knocker. Many a rent man, tallyman or anyone who comes to the house requiring payment has had to 'take it out of Davy Jones's till payday'.

Davy Large   *Barge*
Formed on the name of an ex-docker who later became a union official.

Day & Night   *1 Light (ale)*
Another term for the bottled sunshine

2 Light (illumination)

Upon entering a darkened room one switches on the 'day and night'.

Days a Dawning   *Morning*
A self explanatory and possibly over obvious piece.

Dead Loss   *Boss*
Said by workers of Mr or Mrs Unpopular.

Deaf & Dumb   *Bum*
One of several terms for this part of the anatomy. This applies to both the anus and the buttocks, therefore someone offering anything that is unwanted may be told to 'Shove it up your deaf and dumb'. Or it may be used in glowing terms of reference, e.g., 'She's got a lovely little deaf and dumb.'

Dearie Me   *Three*
An example from the bingo caller.

Deep Sea Diver   *Fiver (£5)*
A contemporary piece that is still in the process of catching on.

Denis Law   *Saw*
A carpenter's term formed on the name of a Scottish international footballer famed for his sharpness in front of goal.

Derby Kelly   *Belly*
Very old and well known, always reduced to 'Derby' or 'Derby Kell'.

Derry Down Derry   *Sherry*
Theatrical piece often reduced to D D D or Three Ds.

Derry & Toms   *Bombs*
Formed on the name of a London store during the blitz. Sadly ironic that the first element should be the name of a place that has seen so many bombs. After 111 years trading in Kensington High Street, Derry and Toms closed down in 1973. The site is now occupied by British Home Stores.

Desperate Dan   *Tan*

Modern term for the desired colour of the sun worshipper or sun bed enthusiast. Formed on the name of the tough guy of a children's comic who gets his tan with a blow torch.

Deuce & Ace *Face*
Shortened to 'deuce' when it is used which is rarely.

D For Dunce *Bunce*
Dislengthened to 'deefer' this applies to money earned on top of regular wages, such as tips, fiddles or cash-in-hand jobs that the taxman will never know about. Hopefully.

Diana Dors *Drawers*
Used jokingly when mentioning women's unmentionables. Named after a British actress (1931–84).

Dick & 'Arry *Dictionary*
An old schoolboy's term that necessitates inclusion.

Dick Emery *Memory*
A man with a bad 'Dick' needn't have a social problem. Based on the British comedian (1917–83).

Dickory Dock *1 Clock*
Old term based on the nursery rhyme.

2 Cock (penis)
Not believed to be responsible for 'dicky' or 'dick' as dick was in existence as a term for the bald headed hermit before this piece was formed.

Dicky Bird *Word*
Not used to describe a written word but signifies a conversation and is always used in full, e.g., 'a dicky bird in your ear'.

Dicky diddle *Piddle*
Rare alternative for JIMMY RIDDLE (qv).

Dicky Dirt *Shirt*
Ancient and extremely well worn piece.

Didn't Ought *Port (wine)*
What good girls supposedly said when asked if they

wanted another. They would nod their heads and refuse.

Diesel Fitter　　*Bitter (Ale)*
Always halved to 'diesel' which could be said to be a fair description of the liquid that is passed off as beer in some premises.

Dig in the Grave　　*Shave*
An old expression for the scraping of the face and always cut down to a 'dig'.

Ding Dong　　*Sing Song*
When this term was coined it applied to a bunch of (usually inebriated) people gathered round a piano singing all those 'good old toons'. It has now evolved into a general party or knees-up, e.g., 'We're having a ding dong round our place on Saturday. Bring a bottle if you want to come and if you don't send the bottle on its own.'

Ding Dong Bell　　*Hell*
Always reduced to 'ding dong' it is mostly used as an expression of surprise and normally follows the F word, e.g., 'Fucking ding dong'.

Dipstick　　*Prick*
An appropriate term when used anatomically but is generally used in reference to a fool.

Dirty & Rude　　*Nude*
What all nakedness was in pre-permissive times and still is to people of that era.

Dirty Daughter　　*Water*
One of several terms with daughter as the second element regarding one of nature's elements.

Dirty Den　　*Pen*
A modern formation based on a character from a TV serial.

Dirty Dick　　*Nick*
Applies to a police station or prison sometimes shortened to 'the dirty'.

Dirty Leper   *Pepper*
Sometimes called 'dirt' which pepper may resemble.

Dirty Old Jew   *Two*
An old bingo caller's term.

Dirty Tyke   *Bike*
One of several terms for the two wheeler.

Dirty Whore   *Four*
Used as a comic reference to £4.

Doctor Crippen   *Dripping*
The infamous murderer hereby gives his name to the infamous toast topping which is to healthy eating what the man was to marriage guidance.

Dog & Bone   *Phone*
A much used term for a much used instrument.

Doctor Who   *Two*
A modern bingo caller's term. From the TV series.

Dog & Cat   *Mat*
An apposite term since either of these pets will make the mat in front of the fire its own property.

Dog & Duck   *Ruck (Fight)*
Probably formed on the name of a pub where fistiknuckles was prevalent.

Dog & Pup   *Cup*
Always reduced to a 'dog' it is what is drunk from or what is played for.

Doggett's Coat & Badge   *Cadge*
See COAT & BADGE.

Dog's Tooth   *Truth*
Employed by way of emphasis, e.g., 'I swear that's the dog's tooth.' Possibly a roundabout way of swearing on the bible since dog is backslang for God.

Dolly Cotton   *Rotten*
Seldom if ever used term for food that has gone off. RS

being what it is, though, she may make a comeback in the guise of Dot Cotton who is a popular TV character.

Dolly Varden

Garden
Formed on the name of a Dickensian character, apart from a back garden it also refers to Covent Garden.

Donald Duck

1 Fuck
Applies to the sexual act and to not caring, e.g., 'I don't give a Donald Duck what you think.'

2 Luck
Always used in full and is often a greeting from one punter to another in the betting shop, i.e., 'how's your Donald Duck?'.

Don't Be Rude

Food
May come from a mother's admonishment, e.g., 'Eat with your mouth shut and don't be rude.'

Do Me Good(s)

Wood(s) (Woodbine)
These were the cigarettes much loved by the British Tommy of World War One. This was used with typical bravado by smokers when cigarettes were linked with cancer.

Doppelganger

Banger
A television scriptwriter's term for a sausage.

Doris Day

1 Gay
Formed on the name of an American singer this modern term applies to homosexuality.

2 Way
To be 'on your Doris' signifies your imminent departure.

Dorothy Squire(s)

Tyre(s)
Always reduced to this singer's Christian name, e.g., a flat Dorothy or a set of Dorothys.

Dot & Carry

Marry
An old example based on a slang expression meaning to walk with a limp, bringing into play the time honoured view of marriage being a handicap.

Dot & Dash   *Tash*
That is a moustache.

Douglas Hurd   *Turd*
A recent term based on the British politician. When a person goes to perform what for a man is a sit down job on the lavatory they have gone to 'dump a Douglas'. Also the one reclining on the pavement waiting to be stepped on.

Dover Harbour   *Barber*
Formed before barbers made the transition to hairdressers and made us pay more for the privilege.

D'Oyly Carte   *1 Fart*
Generally dropped as a 'D'Oyly'.

2 Heart
A term that has obvious relevance to 'eart and is spoken as 'I've got a bit of wind round de oily cart.' A loud artistic burp may follow.

Dribs & Drabs   *Crabs (Crab Lice)*
Said to anyone scratching themselves in the pubic area for whatever reason, 'What's the matter, got the dribs and drabs?'

Drip Dry   *Cry*
Usually shortened to first element, e.g., 'Come on stop "dripping" and tell me what's wrong.'

Drum & Fife   *Knife*
Sometimes known as a 'drummond' and married up with ROAST PORK (qv) whereby a knife and fork becomes a DRUMMOND & ROCE.

Duck & Dive   *Skive*
To avoid work by means of 'ducking and diving' out of sight of manager, foreman or wives.

2 Survive
What a person with no visible means of income has to do.

Duck's Arse   *Grass (Informant)*
A DA is slang for slang. *See* GRASSHOPPER.

Duchess of Fife   *Wife*
Usually refers to that half of a long-married couple and is well known as 'my old dutch'.

Duchess of Teck   *Cheque*
Known as a 'Duchess' and goes arm in arm with her old man. *See* DUKE OF TECK.

Duchess of York   *Pork*
A modern term for pig meat.

Dudley Moore(s)   *Sore(s)*
The comedian and jazz pianist, born on the fringe of the East End, lends his name to an unpleasant condition. Herpes sufferers may break out in 'Dudleys', be it in the form of shingles, a cold sore or otherwise. Applies to any kind of skin eruption.

Duke of Argyll   *File*
Refers to the tool.

Duke of Fife   *Knife*
An old term from the army.

Duke of Kent   *1 Bent*
This applies to all forms of the word. Anything crooked or mis-shapen, such as a nail, a car bumper after a prang, Quasimodo, etc. Also refers to a less than straight person, a bent copper for example, and to homosexuals.

2 Rent
Has a shared popularity with BURTON ON TRENT (qv).

Duke of Teck   *Cheque*
A 'dodgy duke' is a rubber one.

Duke of York   *1 Cork*
That which seals a bottle.

2 Fork
Refers to the implement but is most readily connected to the hands which have long been known as forks. Hence 'Put up your dukes' has become a familiar expression as a fistic challenge.

3 Talk

Less common that RABBIT & PORK (qv) but wasn't always so.

Dull & Dowdy *Cloudy*
An obvious piece in relation to the weather but can also be applied to unclear beer.

Dunkirk *Work*
Scene of a lot of hard work in 1940 and used as in 'I'll see you later, I'm off to Dunkirk.'

Dunlop Tyre *Liar*
A teller of untruths is known as a 'dunlop'.

Dustbin Lid *Kid*
Common and quite popular to call children 'dustbins'. Relevant in most cases too. Incidentally in backslang KID becomes DIK so could the original clever Dick have been the classroom swot, i.e., a clever kid?

Dutch Peg(s) *Leg(s)*
One of several terms for the gams rhyming with 'pegs'.

Dynamite *Fight*
Generally employed in the abbreviated form of 'dyna'.

Earls Court	***Salt*** A less used variant of HAMPTON COURT (qv).
Early Bird	***Word*** Used in the same way as DICKIE BIRD (qv).
Early Doors	***Drawers*** Ancient term that was used mainly in jest.
Early Hour(s)	***Flower(s)*** Old florist's example and an appropriate one since they have to be on the market early to get the best bloomers.
Early Morn	***Horn (Erection)*** An apposite piece since men often wake up in this state but usually a visit to the lavatory takes it down a peg.
Eartha Kitt(s)	***Shit(s)*** A modern term based on the name of an American songstress. It is either to defecate or to have the back door trots.
Earwig	***Twig*** In this case twig means to understand or to catch on.
East & West	***1 Chest*** Only used in an anatomical sense. ***2 Vest*** An elderly reference to underwear.

East India Docks   *Pox (VD)*
Reduced to 'The East India's' and based on one of the old docks of East London.

Eau de Cologne   *Phone*
Always shortened to 'the odour' or 'odie'.

Edgar Britt(s)   *Shit(s)*
Ex-jockey and rival to JIMMY BRITS (qv).

Edna May   *Way*
Employed in exactly the same way as DORIS DAY (qv), based on a music hall artiste and is obviously the older of the two.

Edward Heath   *Teeth*
Formed on the name of the former Prime Minister who was renowned for flashing his gnashers every time he laughed. Known as 'Edwards' sometimes 'Teds'.

2 Thief
Seem to be an untrustworthy lot these ex-tory Prime Ministers (*See* HAROLD MACMILLAN). In this guise the term is normally Ted Heath.

Eels & Liquor   *Nicker (£1)*
Generally termed 'an eels'. In this example the liquor is not the alcoholic kind but the gravy served only in Eel and Pie restaurants.

Egg & Spoon   *Coon*
A derogatory term for a black person.

Eiffel Tower   *Shower*
A peeping Toms delight, an eyeful in the Eifel.

Eighteen Carat   *Claret*
Mainly refers to blood but may also apply to the wine.

Eighteen Pence   *Sense*
Asked of anyone acting pillockishly, 'Ain't you got no eighteen pence?'

Eisenhower   *Shower*
World War Two term after the US general and later Presi-

dent, Dwight D. Eisenhower (1890–1969).

Elephant & Castle

1 Arse Hole
Based on an area of SE London and refers to the channel up which things should be thrust. The things people have told their fellow human beings to 'shove up their elephants' is enough to make even Jumbo's eyes water.

2 Parcel
An example from the post office.

Elephant's Trunk

Drunk
to 'cop an elephant' is the usual parlance for getting kaylied.

Elsie Tanner

Spanner
A 60s term for the nut turner formed on the name of a popular TV character.

Engineers & Stokers

Brokers
An old example for the men who come and snatch back goods for which payment has not been kept up.

English Channel

Panel
This is a reference to the state sickness benefit. People drawing sick pay for 13 consecutive weeks had to appear before a panel of doctors who would decide whether payment could be continued or not.

Enoch Powell

1 Towel
The most common employment for this term based on a British MP.

2 Trowel
Mainly employed by bricklayers. In both cases it is reduced to 'Enoch'.

Epsom Races

Braces
Old and outmoded term.

Errol Flynn

Chin
Anatomical and also to 'take it on the Errol' or take it like a man, based on the controversial Australian film star (1909–59) with a big reputation.

Errol Flynns

Bins

Localized term referring to binoculars which is extended to mean spectacles.

Evening Breeze   *Cheese*
Sometimes known as 'sweet evening breeze'.

Evening News   *Bruise*
Often refers to a love bite which is usually news of the previous evening. Named after a defunct London newspaper.

Everton Toffee   *Coffee*
People have been percolating pots of Everton for well over a hundred years.

Exchange & Mart   *Tart*
This applies to a tart in the guise of a prostitute and is apt since she puts herself on the market. Formed on the name of the weekly paper for those wishing to buy or sell.

Eyes Front   *Cunt*
Used only to call somebody a fool, e.g., 'You eyes front.'

Eyes of Blue   *True*
Used in the context of 'too eyes of blue,' signifying definite agreement. And when telling the absolute truth it becomes '100% eyes of blue, stand on me'.

Fag Packet
1 Jacket
Entry into the best places is forbidden without a 'fag' on.

2 Racket
Applies in all senses of the word, two of which can be used at the Wimbledon tennis championships. Firstly the bat and secondly the prices they charge for the traditional strawberries is a right 'fag packet'. Also applies to a loud noise.

Fainting Fit
Tit(s)
An indelicate example from the lecher.

Fair Enough
Puff (Homosexual)
Could the term 'fairy' come from a reduced form of this, i.e., 'fair e'?

Fairy Story
Tory
Some would say that this exactly represents Conservative election promises. Always employed in the first element giving access to many humorous possibilities, 'Vote fairy', for example.

False Alarm(s)
Arm(s)
Always used in full because any talk of 'falsies', especially in the case of a woman, could be misconstrued.

Family Tree
Lavatory
An old term that is used as 'I'm just going to water the

family tree.'

Fanny Blair *Hair*
An ancient piece that may incorporate the pubic variety.

Fanny Craddock *Haddock*
Applies to the fish on a dish as served up by this culinary expert of TV fame.

Fanny Hill *Pill*
Mainly applies to a contraceptive pill and is based on the book by John Cleland.

Far & Near *Beer*
As ordered at the NEAR AND FAR (qv).

Faraway Place *Case*
Generally a suitcase and probably coined by a holidaymaker who on his return to London found that his luggage was *en route* to Melbourne or Mexico or some other faraway place.

Farmer Giles *Piles*
The 'farmers' is the commonest term in respect of the anal affliction.

Fat & Wide *Bride*
As she may appear in a seaside postcard. May also allude to the belle of a shotgun wedding.

Fat Guts *Nuts*
Only applies to the fruit and implies an over indulgence.

Father O'Flynn *Gin*
An old term based on an old song.

Feather & Flip *Kip (Sleep)*
Used either as to 'get some feather' or as 'going to feather' which means going to bed.

Feather Plucker *Fucker*
Only used in a jocular vein, if a person had a grievance against someone he wouldn't mince words.

Feel Fine *Nine*
'Give me a feel' is a request for £9. Be careful who you ask.

Feet & Yards *Cards*
Refers to playing cards but only applies in the plural. One may have a hand of 'feet' but not a single 'foot'.

Fiddle De Dee *Pee/Wee*
Always slashed to a 'fiddley' and may have something to do with button flies.

Fiddlers Three *Pee/Wee*
A variant of the previous entry that is reduced to a 'fiddlers'.

Field of Wheat *Street*
Nice sarcasm involved here. A dirty, littered, traffic choked street will be pointed out as 'a nice field of wheat'.

Fife & Drum *Bum*
Only used in relation to the buttocks. A naughty child may be threatened with having its fife and drum smacked.

Fifteen Two *Jew*
A piece borrowed from the game of cribbage.

Fighting Fifth *Syph(ilis)*
A term that encompasses all forms of VD.

Fillet of Cod *Sod*
Condensed to the first element as a form of mild admonishment, e.g., 'Come here you little fillet.'

Fillet of Plaice *Face*
Scaled down to 'fillet' this is a variant of the more common KIPPER AND PLAICE (qv).

Fillet of Veal *Steel*
Steel is archaic slang for prison and this is a very old term.

Fine & Dandy *Brandy*

An ancient term that is still around,.

Finger & Thumb

1 Drum
Originally applied to a road, for which drum is a traveller's term, picked up by tramps who would 'hit the finger'. Can also apply to what accompanies the 'old Joanna' down the pub.

2 Mum
Used only in the third party, e.g., 'My old finger's getting on a bit but she's all there with her cough drops.'

3 Rum
An old but quite common piece amongst rum drinkers.

Finsbury Park

Arc (Light)
An example from the technical side of the film business.

Fire Alarms

Arms
A military term for firearms which is also used anatomically, but secondarily.

Fireman's Hose

Nose
Always reduced to the first element, e.g., 'Don't pick your fireman's you'll go bandy.'

First Aid

Blade
Refers to a chiv, i.e. a knife used by a thug. Inspired by the typical retort of a knife wielding villain. 'Can your wife/mum do first aid? Well get her to stitch this up.' It can also refer less menacingly to a razor blade.

First Aid Kits

Tits
Asking a girl to administer first aid takes on a new meaning. Commonly called 'first aids'.

First of May

Say
An old term regarding speaking up for one's self, e.g., 'If you're quite finished I'll have my first of May.'

Fish & Chip(s)

1 Lip(s)
Refers to insolence as well as anatomically in exactly the same way as BATTLESHIP (qv).

2 Tip(s)
A 'fish' is a gratuity.

Fisherman's Daughter

Water
Shortened to 'a drop of fisherman's' this is an old accompaniment of scotch.

Five to Four

Sure
Based on these odds which are short enough to represent a reasonably sure thing. Often said in disbelief at a statement, e.g., 'Are you five to four?', possibly to a racing commentator.

Five to Two

Jew
A racecourse term, based on these odds, where Jews are an integral part of the scene whether as bookmakers or punters.

Flag Unfurled

World
Originally referred to a man of the world but now applies to our planet in general. Aptish I suppose.

Flake of Corn

Horn (Erection)
Waking up with a 'flake on' could signify breakfast in bed.

Flanagan & Allen

Gallon
Used only as a measurement for motor fuel as in price or miles per Flanagan. Formed on the name of a music hall comedy act who were part of the Crazy Gang, Bud Flanagan (1896–1968) and Chesney Allen (1894–1982).

Flash of Light

Sight
Originally applied to anyone who dressed loudly or over the top and looked 'a right flash of light'. Now in reduced form 'flash' has entered the language as a word in its own right, e.g., 'flash' bastards are commonplace.

Flea & Louse

House
Indicative of a seedy place that makes you feel itchy just to look at it. A rundown cinema is known as a flea pit. May also have applied to a brothel.

Flea Bag

Nag
Nothing to do with a verbal assault from the wife but to a scruffy old horse.

Fleas & Lice — *Ice*
Applies to ice as used to chill drinks. It is interesting to see a barmaid's reaction when asked if she has any 'fleas'.

Flounder & Dab — *Cab*
Extremely old term for a taxi which originally referred to a Hansom cab.

Flour Mixer — *Shixa*
A term from Jewish Cockneys that refers to a girl not of their own persuasion.

Flower Pot — *1 Cot*
Where all little seedings get their heads down.

2 Hot
Used almost exclusively in the context of getting a rucking. To 'cop a flower pot' is to 'cop it hot', that is to be severely reprimanded.

Flowery Dell — *Cell*
This is an old term for where the prisoner does his time. Generally contracted to 'flowery'.

Flunkey & Lackey — *Paki*
Always abbreviated to 'flunkey' as a derogatory name for a Pakistani.

Fly by Night — *Tight*
A reference to one who has had a skinful.

Fly By Nights — *Tights*
Modernish term for this type of legwear.

Flying Duck — *Fuck*
A variant of AYLESBURY DUCK (qv). Incidentally, in back-slang the word becomes 'kaycuff' and in the absence of a rhyming term for 'bastard' its back formation, 'dratsab' has to suffice. Therefore if you are called a 'kaycuffing dratsab' by somebody who isn't smiling, it's ruction time.

Fog & Mist — *Pissed*
To be foggy is to have reached a state of inebriation.

Food & Drink   *Stink*
Rarer, but more relevant to the common PEN AND INK (qv).
When the stunning stench of garlic takes up residence in
the bowel, the evidence of its escape will cause the sur-
rounding atmosphere to food and drink like the inside of
an Iraqi tank during the Gulf war.

Fork & Knife   *Life*
Generally used in terms of 'not on your' or 'never in your
fork and knife'.

Forsyte Saga   *Lager*
A modern expression, taken from a classic television
serial, for what is also known as 'maidens' water'.

Four by Two   *Jew*
Once said unkindly to be the average size of a Jewish
nose, in inches presumably. Reduced to 'four-by'.

Fourth of July   *Tie*
A piece brought over by yanks and mainly ignored by
cockneys.

Fox & Hound   *Round*
Applies only to a round of drinks, hence the expression,
'Whose fox and hound is it?'

Francis Drake(s)   *Brake(s)*
Inspired by the man who put the brakes on the Armada
thus ensuring no Englishman would ever have to eat
paella.

France & Spain   *Rain*
Normally abbreviated to 'Frarny'.

Frankie Howerd   *Coward*
The late tittermonger (1917–92) lends his name to the
type of person that he often portrayed on stage and in
films.

Frankie Laine   *Chain*
Formed at the height of this singer's popularity, it refers
to the chain in the toilet. Even though this apparatus has
become a rarity in modern toilets people still 'pull the
Frankie'.

Frankie Vaughan   *Prawn*
Based on the British entertainer in reference to the shellfish.

Fred Astaire   *Hair*
This differs from the ultra familiar BARNET FAIR (qv) in that it applies to individual hairs. You wouldn't find a 'Barnet' in your dinner or on your partner's collar but a 'Fred'. Named after the American entertainer (1899–1987).

Fred Perry   *Jerry*
A bit out of order that the only good tennis player we've ever had should end up under the bed.

French Kiss   *Piss*
Only applies to urination.

French Loaf   *Rofe*
Rofe being four in backslang.

Friar Tuck   *Fuck*
Can be used in a sense of not caring, e.g., 'not to give a friars' or in reference to the sexual act. Prostitutes plying their trade around the old East End would proposition possible clients with 'D'you want a Friar Tuck?' The stock answer was 'I'd sooner fry a sausage.' They may still say it, I don't know. (Honest darling!) Also when taken by surprise in mixed company, 'What the Friar Tuck...?'

Frock & Frill   *Chill*
A reference to a cold.

Frog & Toad   *Road*
One of the most famous terms of RS. Normally shortened to 'the frog'.

Frog in the Throat   *Boat*
Probably is only used among rivermen.

Front Wheel Skid   *Yid*
One of the lesser known pieces for a child of Israel.

Fruit & Nut   *Cut*
Applies to an injury. After a clash of heads, a boxer may complain that, 'He fruit me with his nut.'

Frying Pan

1 Fan
Refers to an admirer. On meeting a favourite performer it may be said, 'I've been a frying pan of yours for years.'

2 Hand
An older application and it matters not about the 'D'. It's never sounded anyway.

Full Moon

Loon
Loon is the condensed version of lunatic although it doesn't apply to being mad but to acting mad, which in some cases amounts to the same thing. Anyone behaving thus will be described as being 'a right full moon' which is apt, as the connection with the moon and madness is legendary.

Fun & Frolics

Bollocks
Refers to testicles and to an unbelievable statement, e.g., 'What a load of fun and frolics you're talking.' Bollocks is a language many people speak fluently. Whenever there is a gathering of people and nobody can think of anything to say someone will invariably state: 'Well, this is fun isn't it?' Now you know what they really mean.

Funny Face(s)

Lace(s)
Applies to shoe or boot laces and is used humorously in warning people whose shoe strings may be undone, e.g., 'Mind you don't trip over your funny face.'

Funny Feeling

Ceiling
Fitting when you've had a few and the lid won't stop spinning.

Fusilier(s)

Ear(s)
One of several terms for the spectacle hangers.

Fusilier

Beer
Ancient but still occasionally heard piece.

Game of Nap　　*1 Cap*
Based on a card game the kitty for which may be collected in this type of headware.

2 Crap
Refers to the act of defecating, e.g., 'Sorry I'm late, I was having a game of nap.'

Garden gate　　*1 Eight*
A bingo term and also £8 is in a 'garden'.

2 Magistrate
Old but still used as in 'going up before the garden'.

Garden gates　　*Rates*
Old term for the old system of payments to local government.

Garden Gnome　　*Comb*
Fairly recent term for the 'flea raker'.

Garden Plant　　*Aunt*
Reduced to 'garden' but only in the third person.

Garibaldi Biscuit　　*Risk It*
On noticing that his lorry was overloaded the driver was heard to remark, 'Well it's only got to go a couple of miles so I'll Garibaldi it.'

Gary Glitter　　*Bitter (Ale)*
Based on the rock'n'roll singer who at one time had a

strong liking for the product. In short a pint of 'Gary'.

Gates of Rome *Home*
Be it ever so humble there's no place like your 'gates of Rome'.

Gavel & Wig *Twig (To Scratch An Itchy Anus)*
To 'have a bit of dirt in your eye' or 'an eyelash twisted' in public can be an intolerable situation. The relieving of this irritation is called twigging or 'having a good old gavel'.

Gay & Frisky *Whisky*
Has sat on the top shelf for a long time.

Gay Gordon *Traffic Warden*
Based on the name of the dance that you might want to do on the grave of the one who gave you that ticket.

General Booth *Tooth*
Based on the name of William Booth (1829–1912) the founder and first general of the Salvation Army. How well off he was in choppers department I know not.

General Election *Erection*
A polite allusion to a standing member.

General Smuts *Nuts (Testicles)*
Reduced to the 'generals' probably to signify their importance. Based on the name of a South African Soldier of the Boer War who later became Prime Minister of that country (1870–1950).

Geoffrey Chaucer *Saucer*
Never heard this in association with a UFO. Flying Geoffreys? Don't see why not. Named after the poet (1342–1400) who is considered the father of English poetry.

George & Ringo *Bingo*
Heard occasionally in the heyday of the Beatles after Messrs Harrison and Starr.

George & Zippy *Nippy*
Very modern term based on the two TV puppets that has nothing to do with Japan but to cold weather.

George Bernard Shaw *Door*
Normally reduced to closing the 'George Bernard'. Based on the Irish wordsmith (1856–1950).

George Blake *Snake*
A totally fitting piece that refers to a person who cannot be trusted. Based on the name of a British traitor.

Georgie Best *1 Guest*
Mainly used in the invitational sense of be my guest, e.g., 'Can I borrow your pen?' 'Please, be my Georgie Best.'

2 Pest
Based on the name of an Irish international footballer and mainly applies to the drunken pest who will not leave you alone while you are trying to enjoy a quiet drink.

George Melly *Belly*
Modern term based on the name of a jazz singing art critic, relating to a paunch.

George Raft *1 Draft*
This is second hand car dealer's parlance for a banker's draft.

2 Draught
An older example than 1 meaning cold air or beer.

3 Graft
A reference to work of a hard nature based on an American actor (1895–1980).

George Robey *Toby*
Originally referred to a road for which toby is an old slang term. Nowadays it is more commonly applied to that brand of beer. Named after the English comedian who was known as the Prime Minister of mirth. Born in 1869, he died Sir George Robey in 1954.

George The Third *Turd*
Applies to that reeking piece of gunge on the pavement that you didn't see. Otherwise you wouldn't have trodden in it.

German Band(s) *Hand(s)*
Always abbreviated to 'Germans' and inspired by the fact

that such musicians were common in London parks in the early part of this century.

German Flute(s) *Boots*
An elderly piece that is now way down the list of terms for footwear.

Gert & Daisy *Lazy*
Based on the stage names of the variety comediennes Elsie and Doris Walters, this is employed in fierce criticism of a slothful person, e.g., 'You could have finished this job hours ago if you weren't so Gert and Daisy.'

Gertie Gitana *Banana*
An old example based on the name of an old music hall turn (1888–1957).

Giggle & Titter *Bitter (Ale)*
Commonly known as 'giggle' and seems to be based on the antics of an over friendly drunk.

Gillie Potter(s) *Trotter(s) (Feet)*
Named after an early radio comedian whose reports from the imaginary town of Hogsnorton made him a popular artiste (1887–1975).

Ginger Ale *Jail*
Shortened to the first element, giving rise to the relevant quote, 'The ginger's full of gingers.' *See next entry.*

Ginger Beer *Queer (Homosexual)*
Widely employed in the cut down form of 'ginger'.

Ginger Pop *Cop (Policeman)*
Generally arrested at the first part and may be connected with an old song, part of which goes:
>*Went down the Lane*
>*To buy a penny whistle*
>*Copper came along*
>*Took me penny whistle*
>*Asked him for it back*
>*Said he hadn't got it*
>*Aye aye ginger nut*
>*You've got it in your pocket.*

Girl & Boy   *1 Saveloy*
An early piece for an early take away.

2 Toy
A later evolvement and a somewhat happy one.

Girls & Boys   *Noise*
An appropriate example given the synonymity of the word with the term.

Give & Take   *Cake*
Not often used but when it is, it is never shortened.

Glasgow Ranger   *Stranger*
Underworld term used by look out men watching for police while the spieler goes through his patter, whether it is selling from a suitcase or inviting people to find the Lady in the three card trick. Generally shortened to a 'Glasgow'.

Glass Case   *Face*
There are many terms for the physog but not many as old as this one.

Glass of Beer   *Ear*
A variant of BOTTLE OF BEER (qv) and employed in the same way.

Glass of Plonk   *Conk (Nose)*
Usually applies to large red varieties which are probably the result of an over bending of the elbow.

Glenn Hoddle   *Doddle (Simple Task)*
During this England international footballer's career with Tottenham Hotspur, the sportswriters of Fleet Street never seemed to tire of the headline 'Doddle for Hoddle'.

Glue Pot   *Twat (Vagina)*
Touching which results in sticky fingers.

Gobstopper   *Chopper (Penis)*
Often used in relation to oral sex. e.g., 'Suck it and see if it changes colour.'

Goddess Diana   *Tanner*
If this coin were still with us it would surely have been re-named 'Princess Diana.'

God Forbid(s)   *1 Kid(s)*
When this piece was coined families on the whole were larger than those of today, when the only birth control people used was a prayer to the Almighty, e.g., 'God forbid we have any more kids.' It was not a successful method.

2 Yid
An obvious term since this is as much a part of Jewish tradition as the Ten Commandments and Matzos. From the silent prayer of the Jewish taxi driver, 'God forbid I should ever forget to put the meter on,' to the re-assurance of the baker, 'God forbid I should ever sell you a stale beigel.'

3 Lid (Hat)
Sometimes used but TIT FOR TAT (qv) is the guvnor in this area. It has been used in reference to a crash helmet (A skid lid) the inference being 'God forbid I should ever need it.'

God in Heaven   *Seven*
An example from the bingo hall.

God Love Her   *Mother*
A piece used in the third person, e.g., 'My old God love her'.

God Save The Queens   *Greens*
A jocular reference to green vegetables and used in full when trying to get the children to eat them.

Golden Hind   *Blind*
Said sympathetically, e.g., 'Bad eyes? She's almost Golden Hind, poor cow.' Inspired by the name of the ship in which Francis Drake plundered the Spanish treasure ships in 1579–80.

Gold Ring   *King*
At present this applies to the playing card but if his mother ever moves over there could be a ready made piece of RS for Charles III.

Gold Watch   *Scotch (Whisky)*
Very common term that is never said in short.

Golliwog   *Dog*
Applies to all mutts but mainly to greyhounds, whereby to go to a dog track is to go to the 'gollies'.

Gone to Bed   *Dead*
Sadly stated, 'Old Sid has gone to bed and he ain't getting up.'

Goodie & Baddie   *Paddy*
Reduced to a 'goodie' in reference to an Irish person.

Goodnight Kiss   *Piss*
The only application for this is urination.

Good Ship Venus   *Penis*
Used poetically and jocularly, often in mixed company. Based on the bawdy song much sung by rugby players.

Goose & Duck   *Fuck*
To 'goose' is to perform the sexual act. Not to be confused with the American 'goose' which means a jab between the buttocks. Can also be used as an expletive when the word may be inappropriate, e.g., 'Goose off', 'Goose me', 'Goosing hell', etc.

Gooseberry Pudding *Woman*
Used as 'the old gooseberry' meaning the wife. This is a geriatric term and even though pudding is always pronounced as pudden it still isn't a good rhyme. But who cares? In backslang the old woman becomes the 'delo nammow'.

Goose's Neck   *Cheque*
Always referred to as 'a goose's'.

Gordon & Gotch   *Watch*
Normally reduced to the first element but rarely used. The main terminology for a watch is a 'kettle'. A red kettle being a gold watch and a white kettle a silver one. Gordon and Gotch was a small firm dealing in books and magazines that operated in Plaistow E13. This must have been a localized term that gained wide usage.

Got out of Pawn   *Born*

Can either be used in full as in the inquiry 'When was you got out of pawn?' Or an expectant father may be asked if his imminent happy event has been 'got out' yet.

Grandfather Clock   *Cock (Penis)*

Often used in conjunction with POLISH AND GLOSS (qv) as a reference to masturbation, e.g., 'She wouldn't go all the way but she didn't mind polishing my Grandfather Clock.'

Granite Boulder   *Shoulder*

Presumably one that can bear a heavy burden.

Grannie Grunt   *Cunt*

No anatomical usage here, an 'old Grannie' refers to someone who is annoyingly sensible or 'old womanish'. The slow driver that you cannot overtake, for example, or the man who had 'better not have a drink or the wife will kill me'.

Grannies Wrinkle(s)   *Winkle(s)*

The seafood known as 'grannies'.

Grape Vine   *Line*

The major employment here is the washing line. Never actually heard of a drowning person being thrown a 'grape'.

Grasshopper   *Copper*

So familiar in the shortened form of 'grass' that it has passed into everyday language for an informant. Still applies, as originally intended, to a policeman but very much secondarily.

Grass in the Park   *Nark (Informer)*

A development of the previous entry.

Grave Digger   *Nigger*

Grave digger is an old slang term for the spade symbol on a playing card. The connection needs no delving into.

Greengage   *Stage*

A theatrical example for the boards that are trodden.

Greengages *Wages*
Mostly referred to as 'greens', for which substitute 'cabbage'.

Green(s) & *Muscle(s)*
Brussel(s) Apt since we are told from an early age that green vegetables make us big and strong.

Gregory Peck *1 Cheque*
The American actor is on first name terms with many a used car dealer.

2 Neck
Has wide usage thanks to television comedies, again mainly in Christian name form.

Grey Mare *Fare*
A term that had its formation before the horseless carriage but still applies to bus and train fares.

Groan and Grunt *Cunt*
A variant of GRUMBLE & GRUNT (qv) used as a derogatory term for women.

Grocer's Shop *Wop*
Fairly recent reference to an Italian.

Grosvenor Squares *Flares*
Used condescendingly by young people when they see anybody wearing this wide bottomed leg wear. Whether it be on a die-hard hippy or their parents' wedding photographs.

Groucho Marx *Sparks (Electrician)*
Usually reduced to 'Groucho' after the American comedian (1890–1977).

Gruesome & Gory *Cory (Penis)*
Always a 'gruesome' probably inspired by the old 'touch it again, it's gruesome more' joke.

Grumble & Grunt *Cunt*
Never used in the form of an expletive but in the reduced form of 'grumble'. Refers to women in general much like crumpet is used. Also refers to that part of a woman that

used to be known as 'Cock Alley' or 'Cock Lane'.

Grumble & Mutter   *Flutter (Bet)*
Inspired by what a losing punter does all the way home from the dog track.

Gunga Din   *Chin*
Based on a character of Rudyard Kipling's creation. The 'gunga' has a fairly wide circulation.

Guzunter   *Punter*
An old and apt term for the bookies' delight. Based on the nickname for a chamber pot which, because it spends its life beneath the bed, is known as a 'goes under'.

Gypsy's Warning   *Morning*
Generally halved to the first element, e.g., 'See you in the gypsy's.'

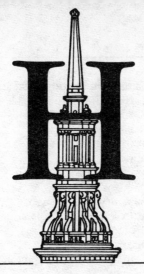

Hackney Marsh(es)   *Glass(es)*
An old term for the drinking vessel but newer in the form of spectacles. Can also apply to binoculars.

Haddock & Cod   *Sod*
Always reduced to the first of this finny pairing and used as a mild expletive. A cheeky child may be called a 'saucy little haddock'.

Hail & Rain   *Train*
An aged piece that has all but run out of track.

Hale & Hearty   *Party*
Apt in that it conjures up visions of healthy enjoyment.

Half a Crown   *Brown*
Heard in a snooker hall concerning the ball of this colour. Half a crown was a coin worth $12\frac{1}{2}$ p in current currency.

Half a Dollar   *Collar*
Said in reduction as 'Arfer' often in connection with a dog's collar. Half a dollar had the same monetary value as the previous entry.

Half a Nicker   *Vicar*
Shortened to 'Arfur' it may be seen as an irreverent reference to his Reverence. Half a nicker is 50p.

Half Inch   *Pinch*

Very familiar in relation to stealing and to a lesser extent being arrested.

Half Ounce   *Bounce (Cheat)*
Anyone thick enough to try to find the lady deserves to be 'half ounced'.

Half Ounce of Baccy   *Paki*
A variant of OUNCE OF BACCY (qv) and reduced to 'half ounce' in reference to a Pakistani child.

Half Ouncer   *Bouncer*
That is the professional ejector.

Half Past Two   *Jew*
One of many terms culminating in 'two' for the chosen one.

Halfpenny Dip   *1 Ship*
Always pronounced 'ha'penny' this was used by London dockers when London had docks.

2 Kip
A recent adaptation to 'have a ha'penny' is to be asleep.

Halfpenny Stamp   *Tramp*
Short changed to a 'ha'penny' which is symbolic of the down and out's financial situation.

Ham & Beef   *Chief*
A prisoner's reference to a chief warder.

Ham & Egg(s)   *Leg(s)*
Usually employed in relation to the shapely female variety.

Ham-bone   *Phone*
Sometimes used as a change from DOG & BONE (qv).

Hammer & Nail   *Tail*
Usually reduced to 'hammer' meaning to follow.

Hammer & Tack   *Back*
An uncommon piece used anatomically.

Hampstead Heath   *Teeth*
Very old but still widely used in the reduced form of 'Hampsteads' or 'Hamps'.

Hampton Court   *Salt*
When asking for the 'Hampton' to be passed be careful not to confuse it with the next item.

Hampton Wick   *Prick (Penis)*
A well known term and one that is unusual in that it can be reduced to both elements. The male member is often referred to as a 'Hampton' indeed Hugh Jampton has been a character in many a comedy sketch. The second half is equally familiar: coitus is known as 'dipping one's wick' and few people realize what the phrase, 'You get on my wick,' actually means. A strange convolution of this has been the emergence of 'Lionel' as a term for man's other best friend. It is derived from Lionel Hampton an American jazz musician.

Ham Shank   *Yank*
A naval term that came about during World War Two.

Handicap   *Clap (VD)*
A supremely pertinent example.

Handley Page   *Stage*
An old theatrical term based on Frederick Handley Page, a pioneering British aircraft designer.

Hand & Fist   *Pissed*
Always used in its full extension.

Hands & Feet   *Meat*
The vegetarian's nightmare, often shrunk to the first element.

Hangar Lane   *Pain*
This is pain in the sense of a nuisance or an annoyance and is a diminutive of a pain in the neck or arse. The term is appropriate because Hanger Lane is a notorious road junction in west London where traffic jams are the norm.

Hansel & Gretel   *Kettle*

In old cockney sculleries the 'Hansel' was always on the go.

Happy Hour(s)   *Flower(s)*
A suspicious look may follow when a gift of 'happy hours' is given to the wife for no reason.

Harbour Light   *Right*
Applies exclusively to correctness. If everything is all right it is referred to as 'all harbour light' and often 'all harbour'.

Hard Hit   *Shit*
To go for a 'hard hit' is to defecate.

Hard Labour   *Neighbour*
Could be regarded as appropriate since a high percentage of 'them next door' are hard work to get on with.

Hare & Hound   *Round*
An exact variation of FOX & HOUND (qv). Both terms are more likely to be based on names of pubs rather than any so called country sport.

Harold Lloyd   *Celluloid*
An old underworld piece for an instrument used for housebreaking. Named after an early film comedian (1893–1971).

Harold Macmillan   *Villain*
Reduced to an 'Arold whereby an ex-Prime Minister becomes a baddie (1894–1986).

Harold Pinter   *Splinter*
An older version of ALAN MINTER (qv) which first caused pain in a timber yard. Always cut to an ''Arold' after the writer of arty plays. But then one man's art is another man's confusion. But what do I know?

Harry Bluff   *Snuff*
Used to be quite common, but then so did snuff.

Harry Huggins   *Muggins (Idiot)*
Normally said in self admonishment for letting somebody get away with something. A foreman may prevent a

worker form sneaking off early because, 'If you get caught who'll cop a bollocking? Harry Huggins here.'

Harry Lime   **_Time_**
Based on a fictional film character it refers to the time of day, e.g., 'What's the Harry Lime?'

Harry Lauder   **_Warder_**
Prisoner's term for a prison officer.

Harry Lauders   **_1 Borders_**
Theatrical term for stage hangings. Also what soldiers of the Border Regiment called themselves. Formed on the name of a Scottish entertainer who was knighted in 1919 for his contribution to the war effort.

2 Orders
A publican may bellow those three terrible words, 'Time gentlemen, please', or 'Last Harry Lauders'. Also what should be obeyed.

Harry Monk   **_Spunk (Semen)_**
Always comes down to 'Harry'.

Harry Randall   **_1 Candle_**
Formed in the days when candles were a constant source of light and not just brought out during power cuts.

2 Handle
As old as (1) and based on the name of a music hall comedian (1860–1932).

Harry Tagg(s)   **_Bag(s)_**
Originally actors' jargon for luggage, it now also applies to trousers for which bags is old slang. Often called ''Arolds'.

Harry Tate   **_1 Eight_**
A bingo caller's term and also refers to £8.

2 Late
Whilst waiting for a long overdue minicab it may be said: 'Look at the time. It'll be too bleeding Harry to go in a minute.'

3 Mate
The first officer in the Merchant Navy.

4 Plate
On which a flustered person may have enough.

5 State
Applies to a state of nervousness or excitement, e.g., 'in a right old Harry Tate'. The ubiquitous Mr Tate was a British comic of the early 20th century who was born in 1872 and died of injuries sustained in an air raid in 1940.

Harry Tate(s)   *Weights*
A reference to a brand of cigarettes.

Harry Wragg   *Fag*
The name of this ex-jockey will live on for as long as people smoke cigarettes.

Harvest Moon   *Coon*
An abusive term for a black person.

Harvey Nichol(s)   *Pickle(s)*
Relates to being in a predicament, e.g., 'in a bit of an Harvey Nichol.' When pluralized it obviously applies to the savoury preserves.

Has Beens   *Greens*
Refers to green vegetables, presumably those that have been boiled to a pulp.

Hat & Coat   *Boat*
Often applied to a refrigerated cargo ship, the unloading of which required a docker to wear his hat and coat.

Hat & Feather   *Weather*
Chiefly used in its full extension, e.g., 'When's this poxy hat and feather gonna clear up?' Sometimes used as 'hatton' as humorous banter:
What's the hatton like?
Raining.
Well I'd better put my hatton.

Hat & Scarf   *Bath*
Can't really see the relevance of this. Who wears a scarf in the bath?

Haystack   *Back*
Applies anatomically and in reference to the rear, e.g., 'tradesman's entrance round the haystack'.

Heap of Coke   *Bloke*
'A heap big heap', as Geronimo would have described his biggest brave had he come from Bow.

Hearts of Oak   *Broke*
Refers to being financially devastated.

Heaven & Hell   *1 Shell*
A wartime term relating to a projectile.

2 Smell
Usually applies to a bad smell that 'don't half heaven!'

Heavens Above   *Love*
A happy example when applied to a new romance. People are not quite earth-bound when they are in 'Heavens above'.

Hedge & Ditch   *Pitch*
A playing area or where a stall holder or bookmaker may set up shop.

Hedgehog   *Wog*
An example from the xenophobe who maintains that all 'hedgehogs' start at Calais.

Helter Skelter   *Shelter*
Originally an air raid shelter in which form it is now thankfully obsolete except in older people's reminiscences. Still occasionally heard in relation to a bus shelter.

Henry Meville   *Devil*
An ancient example and employed in terms of, 'Who the Henry Meville's that knocking at this time of night?'

Henry Nash   *Cash*
An elderly piece that doesn't appear to have been saved.

Here & There   *Chair*
Never shortened, e.g., 'Pull up a here and there and have

a bite to eat.'

Herman Fink   *Ink*
A term that was originally drawn up in the theatre.

Herring & Kipper   *Stripper*
Always reduced to the first element and since strip shows
have moved from clubs to pubs, suggestions to go to one
have been rebuffed with, 'No. I don't want to see some
old herring taking her clothes off. Let's go for a quiet
pint.'

Hide & Seek   *Cheek*
Never shortened and used light heartedly to anyone
trying to take advantage, e.g., 'You've got some hide and
seek, you have!'

Hi Diddle Diddle   *1 Fiddle*
This refers to gaining by dishonest means and is said as
'to be on the hi diddle diddle'. It may take the form of
petty larceny at the work place or a much grander tax
fiddle.

2 Middle
Of a dart board mainly. Nearest to the 'hi diddle diddle'
throws first.

High as a Kite   *Tight*
In its original sense this applied to being drunk but
people who do not realize that being 'high' was reduced
RS took the word into the world of drugs.

Highland Fling   *Sing*
Post war term found on a Billy Cotton record called 'The
Marrow Song' with vocals by Alan Breeze, the band's resi-
dent 'Highland Flinger'.

High Noon   *Spoon*
A 50s term named after the classic western film.

High Stepper   *Pepper*
This term, now a seasoned campaigner, is old slang for a
fashionable person.

Hi Jimmy Knacker   *Tobacco*

This refers to pipe or rolling tobacco, and is inspired by the name of a street game of the distant past.

Hill & Dale　　*Tale*
This applies to the tale of a con artist or beggar in an effort to separate a mark from his money.

Hillman Hunter　　*Punter*
Applies mainly to a client or customer of a prostitute or moody sales persons who sell kitchens and double glazing over the telephone. The term, being an old type of car, was originated not surprisingly by used car salesmen.

Hit & Miss　　*1 Kiss*
By which 'kiss me' masochistically becomes 'hit me'.

2 Piss
Can be used in regard of urine or booze. One can go 'for a' or 'on the hit and miss'.

Hit & Run　　*Done*
Mainly refers to being swindled. If you've been taken, you've been 'hit and run'.

Hobber de Hoy　　*Boy*
Mostly used in full and frequently pronounced 'hibber de hoy' it applies to an adolescent, often one of the hooligan element.

Hobson's Choice　　*Voice*
Very common in reduced form of 'Hobson's'.

Hole in the ground　　*Pound*
Shortened to a 'hole' in reference to £1.

Holler & Shout　　*Kraut (German)*
Appropriate since Germans seem to get a bit loud especially around Spanish swimming pools ... until somebody mentions the war.

Holler Boys Holler　　*Collar*
Originally referred to the detachable collar of a bygone age. Always known as a 'holler boys' and still is. Based on a line in a poem denigrating Guy Fawkes.

Holy Friar   *Liar*
Never shortened, always used light heartedly. You wouldn't call someone who has defamed you a 'holy friar'. You would call him a liar.

Holy Ghost   *1 Post*
A racing term for the starting post, e.g., 'The runners are at the holy.'

2 Toast
Normally cut to 'a slice of holy'.

Holy Nail   *Bail*
A term used by characters of the underworld. Well, nobody else would need to use it would they?

Holy Smoke   *Coke*
Originally the fuel but now applies to the drink.

Holy Water   *Daughter*
The apple of her father's eye is his little holy water.

Honey Pot   *Twat (vagina)*
As possessed by the sexually alluring woman who attracts men like bees round a honey pot.

Hong Kong   *Pong*
Not sure if this is apt because I've never been there, but pong is Chinese for smell isn't it?

Hop It & Scram   *Ham*
A localized piece that is usually sliced to 'hop it'.

Hopping Pot   *Lot*
A widely used term that is nearly always contracted to the first element. 'That's your hopping,' means, 'That's you lot, there's no more.'

Horse & Carriage   *Garage*
Where to fill up your metaphoric horse and carriage when it becomes thirsty.

Horse & Cart   *1 Fart*
Normally employed in the past tense or after the horse has bolted so to speak, e.g., 'What dirty swine's horse &

carted?'

2 Start
A mocking remark to a motorist having ignition problems was 'Won't horse and cart? Get a horse and cart.'

Horse & Trap

1 Clap (VD)
Never shortened always a dose of the 'horse and trap'.

2 Crap
Less common form of PONY & TRAP (qv).

Horse & Trough

Cough
Whereby one may have a nasty 'horse'.

Horse Piddle

Hospital
Not so much RS as a play on words.

Horses & Carts

Darts
Always curtailed to 'horses'.

Horse's Hoof

Poof (Homosexual)
A less frequently employed version of IRON HOOF (qv).

Hot & Cold

Gold
Mainly used in the truncated form of 'hot' often in reference to a piece of jewellery sold on the cheap. Which it most likely is.

Hot Cross Bun

Gun
Only really used for comic effect. Hard to imagine a security guard feeling threatened by the words, 'Don't move, there's a hot cross bun aimed at your head.'

2 Run
To be on the hot cross is to be on the run from the police. Or the wife.

3 Son/Sun
Unusual in either of these settings.

Hot Dinner

Winner
The racing world's alternative to CHRISTMAS DINNER (qv) suggesting that a good meal follows a good result.

Hot Potato

Waiter
An efficient waiter usually as opposed to COLD POTATO (qv).

Hot Toddy   *Body*

This refers to the body beautiful and is inspired by the name of a hot alcoholic drink that is nice to go to bed with on a cold night. The connection is obvious.

Hounslow Heath   *Teeth*

An archaic example that was overtaken in the gnasher stakes years ago.

Housemaid's Knee(s)   *1 Keys*

Usually referred to as a bunch of 'housemaids'.

2 Sea

Modern equivalent of COFFEE AND TEA (qv).

House of Fraser   *Razor*

Generally shaved to a 'Howser' and normally applies to a razor used as a weapon although it can be used innocuously. Based on the retailing chain.

House of Lords   *Cords*

A reference to corduroy strides.

Housewives' Choice *Voice*

Based on a long running radio request programme of yesteryear. This applies to the shrill, raucous voice of a shrieking woman especially a mother noisily castigating a naughty child.

Housey Housey   *Lousey*

To feel 'housey housey' is to feel horribly itchy all over.

How D'ye Do   *1 Shoe*

A very old reference to a chimney holder. *See* CHIMNEY AND SOOT.

2 Stew

Nothing to do with food but to a state of difficulty or mental agitation, e.g., 'I was in a right old how d'ye do. I gets all the way up north for the semi-final and some bastard nicks my money and my ticket.'

Hugs & Kisses   *Missus*

Hardly complimentary to refer to a wife as 'the ugs' but it is meant to be.

Husband & Wife   *Knife*
Normally cut to the first element.

Hush Puppy   *Yuppie*
A derogatory term for these high earning, high profile types, many of whom 'colonized' some parts of the East End, mainly the new docklands development, where once they would have feared to tread.

Hyde Park   *1 Mark*
A theatrical piece for an actor's mark.

2 Nark (Informer)
Variant of CAR PARK (qv).

Ian Rush

Brush
A piece formed in the 80s, on the name of a Welsh international footballer, by a decorator in relation to a paint brush.

Ice Cream Freezer

Geezer
Always melted down to 'ice cream' often used insultingly.

Ideal Home

Comb
An ironic term in that in an ideal home it wouldn't keep getting mislaid.

I'm Afloat

1 Boat
A very old and obvious term.

2 Coat
Equally old as (1) and applies to a heavy winter coat. Often reduced to 'Ima'.

I'm So Frisky

Whisky
Usually nipped to 'I'm so'.

In & Out

1 Snout
Applies to both the nose and to a cigarette.

2 Stout
Refers not to size but that which comes in a bottle.

3 Tout
originally referred to a person who made a living selling

tips to racecourse punters. Now, also, applies to a seller of exorbitantly priced tickets at any venue.

Inky Smudge *Judge*
The man of law who will officially blot your copybook.

In the Mood *Food*
A hungry person is 'in the mood for some in the mood'. Sometimes jokingly changed to:

In the Nude *Food*
Maybe something to do with love bites.

Insects & Ants *Pants*
Refers to underpants and, in brief, 'insects'.

Irish Jig *Wig*
An 'Irish' is an obvious and much ridiculed vanity shield.

Irish Stew *1 True*
Employed in the same manner as EYES OF BLUE (qv), e.g., 'too Irish stew' or for emphasis 'too bloody Irish'.

2 Blue
Refers to all things blue including melancholia.

Iron Duke *Fluke*
A term used in snooker to signify a lucky shot.

Iron Hoof *Poof*
Supremely common piece that is generally minced to the first element.

Iron Hoop *Soup*
A term based on a plaything of a bygone era that has now been rolled into oblivion.

Iron Horse *1 Course*
A reference to a race course.

2 Toss
Pronounced 'torse' this means to toss a coin to settle an issue, e.g., 'All right I'll iron you for it. Heads I drink tails you drive.'

Iron Tank   *Bank*
A term that is symbolic of strength.

Isabella   *Umbrella*
An archaic piece that is probably worn out.

Isle of Man   *Pan*
An example that is never shortened, e.g., 'Bung some bangers in the Isle of Man and I'll butter the Nat King Coles' (qv).

Isle of Wight   *1 Right*
Applies in terms of direction and correctness.

2 Tight
Refers to those people who are not easily parted from their money and to drunkenness.

I Suppose   *Nose*
An ancient piece that is still running.

Itch & Scratch   *Match*
The cheapest form of ignition is a 'box of itches'.

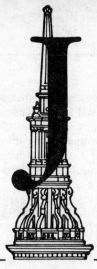

Jack-A-Dandy *Brandy*
Based on an alternative name for Will o' the Wisp which itself is the common name for ignis fatuus. This is the phosphorescent light, caused by the spontaneous combustion of gases emitted by rotting organic matter, that can be seen hovering over swampy ground at night.

The term is probably inspired by the way brandy burns when ignited. On a Christmas pudding for example.

Jack & Danny *Fanny*
A coarse term for the female pudend.

Jack & Jill *1 Bill*
This applies to hate mail, that is mail that we hate to receive, e.g., gas, phone, electric, etc. It also refers to a receipt and is sometimes employed in connection with the police.

2 Hill
Since this is what this couple went up it would appear to be an appropriate if not obvious example.

3 Pill
A piece in everyday use among drug users.

4 Till
A term used by betting shop workers in reference to a cash register. It is also used by those members of the criminal fraternity who make a living by stealing from them.

Jackanory   *Story*
Refers obviously to that which is told to a child but is mainly used in the sense of a lie. A person who lies or tells tall stories in order to impress 'doesn't half tell Jackanorys'. In the same vein an obvious fabrication is often met with, 'Don't give me all that old Mother Hubbard,' i.e., 'Don't tell fairy stories.'

Jack Benny   *Penny*
A term, based on an American comedian (1894–1974), that didn't survive decimalization.

Jackdaw   *Jaw*
Employed anatomically and also to scold. To 'cop a jackdaw' is to be told off.

Jackdaw & Rook   *Book*
A reference from the acting profession.

Jacket & Vest   *West*
The 'jacket' is a reference to the West End of London.

Jack Flash   *Crash/Smash*
Refers to a road traffic accident, e.g., 'There's been another Jack Flash on the M25.' Possibly an allusion to a speeding motorist.

Jack Frost   *Lost*
Refers to a ignorance of whereabouts, e.g., 'If this isn't the B229 I'm Jack Frost.' Also said in disgust whilst tearing up yet another betting ticket, 'Bloody Jack Frost again.'

Jack Horner   *Corner*
Applies to what may be stood in, turned around or cut. Sometimes called the 'little Jack Horner'.

Jack-in-the-Box   *Pox (VD)*
Invariably reduced to the first element.

Jack Jones   *Alone*
Very well known piece and generally shortened to 'on your Jack'.

Jack Malone   *Alone*
Sometimes used instead of JACK JONES (qv) possibly be-

cause it rhymes better.

Jack of Spades   *Shades (Sunglasses)*
In short, 'Jacks'.

Jack Randle   *Candle*
The name of a 19th century prize fighter burns on with this archaic term.

Jacks Alive   *Five*
The commonest term for £5 is a 'Jacks'.

Jack Sprat   *1 Brat*
A precocious or unpleasant child is a 'right little Jack Sprat'.

2 Fat
Cut the 'Jack Sprat' from the bacon in a greasy spoon sandwich and you won't be left with much between the slices.

Jack Tar   *Bar*
A harbour or riverside bar presumably.

Jack the Lad   *Bad*
Descriptive of something no longer fresh, e.g, 'This Jack the Ripper is Jack the lad.' *See next item.*

Jack the Ripper   *1 Kipper*
Well known piece based on the infamous Whitechapel murderer.

2 Slipper
Of secondary employment and was used by schoolboys when corporal punishment was the norm.

Jamaica Rum   *Thumb*
Only heard this used by a disgruntled motorist who had broken down in the middle of nowhere and had to hitch a lift or have it on his 'old Jamaica'.

James Hunt   *Front*
This refers to confidence, whereby a person may have 'more James Hunt than Brighton'. It applies to boldness or just bare faced cheek and is based on the British racing driver.

Jam Jar

Car
The original meaning of this widely used piece was a tram car.

Jam Roll

1 Dole
This is a reference to unemployment and is used as 'being on the jam roll'. Probably based on the fact that a roll and jam is on the menu of many a jobless person.

2 Parole
An underworld term for the conditional discharge from prison.

Jam Tart

1 Sweetheart
Originally applied to a girlfriend but somewhere along the line the jam got eaten and tart became a byword for women in general.

2 Heart
Has been used anatomically but its main usage is towards the suit in a pack of cards.

Jane Russell

Mussel
The name of the American film star is taken for seafood, popular in pubs of a Sunday lunchtime.

Jane Shore

Whore
Based on the name of the mistress of Edward VI and always condensed to a 'Jane'.

Jar of Jam

1 Pram
Put this down to the fact that whenever a clean baby is put in a pram somehow it always manages to get sticky.

2 Tram
An elderly example that when faced with extinction made the transition to (1).

J Arthur Rank

1 Bank
In this sense the term is probably obsolete, its demise due to the popularity of:

2 Wank (Masturbate)
Employed extensively in the dislengthened form of 'J Arthur'. Based on the name of the British film producer and entrepreneur who became Lord Rank (1888–1972).

J Carroll Naish   *Slash*
A reference to urination that is curtailed to 'J Carroll' and called after an American actor (1900–73).

Jekyll & Hyde   *Snide*
Very pertinent in the sense of being two faced. Also refers to fake or counterfeit goods. A copied painting, a moody Rolex, a dodgy bank note. They're all 'Jekylls'.

Jekyll & Hydes   *Strides*
Refers to trousers or jeans.

Jellied Eel(s)   *Wheel(s)*
Applies not only to an actual wheel but to transport in general. 'Have you got jellied eels?' means, have you got means of transport?

Jellybone   *Telephone*
A localized term used by some courier controllers.

Jem Mace   *Face*
An archaic piece based on the name of a 19th century bare knuckle boxing champion (1831–1910).

Jenny Hill(s)   *Pill(s)*
A term of medication based on a music hall performer of the 19th century who never made it to the 20th (1851–96).

Jenny Lee   *1 Flea*
A term that was once as widespread as the parasite.

2 Key
These days this is 'Jenny' at her commonest.

3 Tea
Once enjoyed wide usage but has been upstaged by ROSIE LEE (qv).

Jenny Lind(y)   *Wind(y)*
Can apply to the weather or internal gases that work their way out in one way or another. The lady was a Victorian singer known as 'The Swedish Nightingale', so popular in London that the House of Commons was without a quorum three times because so many MPs had gone to see her and crowds blocked the street outside her home.

An extended form of her name (Jenny Linder) is an ancient term for a window.

Jenny Wren *Ben (Truman)*
Downed to a 'pint of Jenny' in reference to this brand of beer.

Jeremiah *Fire*
Applies to the domestic fire which once would have been exclusively a coal fire. It was common to 'put another piece of merry on the jerry'. *See* MERRY OLD SOUL.

Jeremy Beadle *Needle*
Used in the sense of annoyance and is aptly based on the name of television's arch practical joker whose main aim in life is apparently to give some poor unsuspecting soul a heart attack.

Jericho *Po*
Named after an ancient city that was the scene of a biblical demolition job. Gideon, the leader of the Israelites, in order to save money, brilliantly hired some musicians (whose hourly rate was less than that of the navvies of the day) to blow their trumpets and bring down the walls. Thus revealing many a hapless Canaanite sitting with fingers in ears on their decorous chamber pots midway through fear induced defecation. When they were cleaned these pots became prized spoils of war and became known as jerries.

This story was told to me by a direct descendant of Gideon who had many such family heirlooms. Due to circumstances however he was forced to sell them from the back of a van on some waste ground off the Mile End Road. Not for ten pounds, not for eight, not even six. But to you and I'm robbing myself ....

Jerry-Cum-Mumble *1 Tumble*
This is an extremely ancient piece and in its original sense it meant to tumble over. It later became widely used as 'Jerry' meaning to understand.

2 Rumble
To find out.

Jerry Lee *Pee/Wee*

Based on the name of an American rock'n'roll singer and pianist Jerry Lee Lewis.

Jiggle & Jog   *Frog*
A fairly modern piece for a French person.

Jim Brown   *Town*
An old term for the West End of London.

Jimmy Brits   *Shits*
Reduced to the 'Jimmys' meaning diarrhoea and formed on the name of a British boxer.

Jimmy Grant   *Immigrant*
On its formation in the 19th century this meant emigrant referring to those leaving for the colonies. In Australia, however, the term was rearranged to mean a new arrival.

Jimmy Hill(s)   *Pill(s)*
Based on the name of a television football pundit and ex-player this refers to what may be prescribed or to illicit drugs.

Jimmy Logie   *Bogie (Nasal Residue)*
Formed on the name of an Arsenal footballer of the 50s.

Jimmy Mason   *Basin*
Although it can mean the receptacle its main usage is the same as CHARLIE MASON (qv).

Jimmy O'Goblin   *Sovereign*
Not HM but a pound. Seldom used, but 'Sov' is still popular.

Jimmy Riddle   *Piddle*
Long running and very common piece.

Jimmy Young   *1 Bung*
A backhander or bribe and shortened to the Christian name, e.g., 'I gave the gatekeeper a Jimmy so we'll be alright.'

2 Tongue
Aptly based on the name of a radio personality who ob-

viously does a lot of talking, hence, 'Stop flapping your Jimmy' means keep quiet.

Jim Prescott   *Waistcoat*
An alternative to CHARLIE PRESCOTT (qv).

Jim Skinner   *Dinner*
After a heavy bevvy a man went home drunk and demanding his 'Jim Skinner'. His wife threw a pork chop at him causing him to stagger back, trip over the dog and smack his head heavily against the door frame. 'Thanks love,' he smiled. 'But I won't bother with the vegetables.'

Joanna   *Piano*
A classic piece that always seems to be prefixed with 'old', e.g., 'The party will liven up when Bill starts playing the old Joanna.'

Joan of Arc   *1 Lark*
Not really used in relation to playing about but said after a narrow escape or if in a difficult situation, e.g., 'Sod this for a Joan of Arc'. Had the maid of Orleans been the maid of West Ham she would no doubt have said it herself when they lit the fire.

2 Park
Even in the best kept Joan of Arc there's a piece of dog's shit. A cockney cynicism.

Jockey's Whip   *Kip*
To snatch a little bit of 'jockeys' is to have forty snoozewinks.

Jodrell Bank   *Wank (Masturbate)*
An extensively used example based on the giant observatory in Cheshire.

Joe Blake   *1 Stake*
Sometimes used in betting shops for money that is gambled. Could also be Count Dracula's nemesis.

2 Steak
A term that is not the least bit rare.

Joe Brown   *Town*
A very old example that was possibly coined by

travellers.

Joe Goss   *Boss*
An old piece formed on the name of a 19th century pugilist.

Joe Gurr   *Stir*
An old reference to prison.

Joe Hook   *Crook*
Hook is an old slang term for steal so this most commonly applies to a thief, a dealer in 'hookey gear'.

Joe Hunt   *Cunt*
Generally employed in reference to a fool and often reduced to a 'Joey'. It is also used to describe a less than nice person and in this guise it is never shortened, e.g., 'Wait till you met the new foreman, he's a right Joe Hunt.'

Joe Loss   *Toss*
Based on the name of a British bandleader this can either be used in the sense of not caring, 'I couldn't give a Joe Loss', or to decide an outcome by Joe Lossing a coin.

Joe Ronce   *Ponce*
A reference to a prostitute's minder.

Joe Rook   *Crook*
A variant or maybe a mis-said version of JOE HOOK (qv).

Joe Rourke   *Fork*
This means fork in the guise of a hand but more specifically a hand of a dip. A Joe Rourke is, therefore, a pickpocket.

Joe Savage   *Cabbage*
An ancient term for the vegetable.

Joe Soap   *Dope*
Employed in the same way as his partner HARRY HUGGINS (qv).

John Bull   *1 Full*
Anything from a stadium to a stomach can be 'John Bull'

but the main usage is in reference to being full of alcohol.

2 Pull
Mainly used in reference to being stopped by the police. Also to 'go on the John Bull' is to go out looking for company of the opposite sex.

John Dillon — *Shilling*
A defunct piece for the old monetary unit based on the name of a race-horse.

Johnny Cash — *Slash (Urinate)*
A Johnny-come-lately term based on an American country and western singer.

Johnny Horner — *Corner*
An oft used alternative to JACK HORNER (qv).

Johnny Rollocks — *Bollocks*
Tommy's (qv) rival for what in backslang is 'skollobs'

Johnny Walker — *Talker*
Refers to trappy people, sometimes an informer, but mainly to people who talk incessantly and drive you mad. The connection between the term and loose tongues is obvious.

John O'Groat — *Coat*
Makes no difference that the 's' is missing, this is an old term.

John O'Groats — *Oats (Sexual Satisfaction)*
Commonly used as 'having your John O'Groats'.

John Peel(s) — *Eel(s)*
Applies to jellied eels, a culinary tradition of working class Londoners.

Joint of Beef — *Chief*
A reference to the boss man, e.g., 'Who's the joint of beef around here?'

Jolly Joker — *Poker*
Strangely not the card game but the implement for poking

a fire

Jolly Roger   *Lodger*
A seldom used piece now that 'the old Jolly Roger' is an endangered species.

Joy Stick   *Prick (Penis)*
Not too sure if this is rhyming slang or a description but since it does rhyme it is included. Only applies anatomically.

Judy & Punch   *Lunch*
A modern term because older people do not have lunches. The midday meal break is dinner time. Normally reduced to 'Judy'.

Jug & Pail   *Jail*
The reduced form is not responsible for jug which is a byword for prison. It comes from an old Scottish word 'Joug' meaning pillory. The term, however, does seem quite suitable.

Julius Caesar   *1 Cheeser*
A Cheeser is the diminutive of a Cheese Cutter which is a flat cap

2 Freezer
Interesting that the term for what can make ice cream should be based on an Italian. Perhaps he was the original Okey Pokey Man. No. You're probably right.

Jumbo's Trunk   *Drunk*
An infrequent variant of ELEPHANT'S TRUNK (qv).

Jumping Jack   *Black*
A reference to a black person and sometimes to a black snooker ball.

Just As I Feared   *Beard*
Always trimmed to a 'just as'.

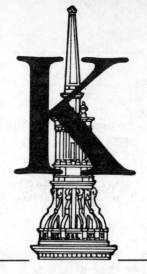

Kangaroo

1 Jew
A widely used term often in regard to on course Jewish bookmakers. Especially in the jumping season it would appear.

2 Screw
A well known reference to a prison officer and secondarily applies to wages.

Kate Carney

Army
Known as 'the Kate' and based on the name of a music hall artiste (1869–1950), this was coined by soldiers of World War One.

Keith Moon

Loon
A 60s example based on a rock drummer (1947–78) whose outrageous exploits led to him being known as 'Moon the loon'. This is a piece that wrote itself.

Ken Dodd

Wad
Refers to a large roll of banknotes produced from the pocket. Or from under the stairs of a house in Knotty Ash. Named after a British comedian who fell foul of the tax man.

Ken Dodds

Cods (Testicles)
'Kick him in the Ken Dodds' (or Kenny's) is an instruction to fight dirty.

Kennington Lane

Pain

Named after a road in south London near the Oval cricket ground, whereby a batsman, facing a West Indian fast bowler without his protective cup, may end up reeling in Kennington Lane.

Kentish Town   *Brown*
A nearby rival to CAMDEN TOWN (qv) in relation to copper coinage.

Kermit The Frog   *Bog (Lavatory)*
Named after a character from the TV series 'The Muppett Show', this is obviously of fairly recent derivation. Nevertheless, there seems to be quite a few people hopping to the 'Kermit' when the need arises.

Kerry Packer(s)   *Knacker(s)*
Based on the name of an Australian entrepreneur and applies, often in the reduced form of 'Kerry's', to the testicles.
   Also employed in relation to being tired, worn-out or no longer functional. A person, an old boot or a car engine can be 'Kerry Packered'.

Kettle on the Hob   *Bob*
This is one of an élite band of male Christian names to have a piece of RS. Always condensed to 'Kettle' but not very often these days. A shilling was also known by this name.

Khyber Pass   *Arse*
A very familiar piece that has almost gained respectability. An oft used expression to get someone going is, 'Give him a kick up the Khyber.'

Kidney Punch   *Lunch*
Always truncated to 'a bit of kidney' often in reference to a pie and a pint.

Kidstake   *Fake*
To be at the kidstakes is to be on the wind up, i.e., to try to con or kid someone by means of a phoney story.

Kilburn Priory   *Diary*
Notably that of a policeman.

Kilkenny

Penny

A spent reference to a coin of a previous currency.

King Canute(s)

Boot(s)

A seldom used variant of the perennial DAISY ROOT(S) (qv).

King Death

Breath

An old expression for halitosis is 'bad king death'.

King Dick

Brick

An old example from the building site.

King Dickie

Brickie

Bricklayers have probably revelled in this term for years.

King Lear

1 Ear

Often used in connection with people on the cadge which is known as being on the ear'ole or on the 'King Lear'.

2 Queer (Homosexual)

An elderly theatrical piece. The term, that is.

King(s) & Queen(s)

Bean(s)

Mainly refers to baked beans whereby 'kings on holy ghost' is a common pairing.

Kings Head

Shed

Although for many men a garden shed is their place of retreat, for many it is where the tools live and so symbolizes jobs that need doing. For these men this is a term of wishful thinking, 'If you want me I'll be down the kings head.'

King's Proctor

Doctor

An uncommon if not obsolete piece. The quack or sawbones will usually suffice.

Kipper & Bloater

1 Motor

A later equivalent of YARMOUTH BLOATER (qv).

2 Photo

Applies to all types of photograph from the holiday snap to 'dirty kippers'.

Kipper & Plaice   *Face*
Always decreased to the first element, often to a moosh of no great beauty, e.g., 'He's got a kipper like a piece of second hand chewing gum.'

Kiss & Cuddle   *Muddle*
Never shortened, to be in a 'right old kiss and cuddle' is to be in a state of confusion.

Kiss Me Hardy   *Bacardi*
The reputed last words of Lord Nelson taken in jocular vein. Whether it is condensed to 'kiss me' or not depends on the sex of the bar person.

Kiss Me Quick   *Prick*
More likely to be associated with a twerp than the male member. Based on the fact that on a beano there is always one person who dons a 'kiss me quick' hat and behaves like a complete pillock. Such a person is a 'kiss me'.

Kiss Of Life   *Wife*
Used by the man whose liver has been saved by marriage.

Kitchen Range   *Change*
Always curtailed to 'kitchen' in relation to what is never checked by men buying drinks.

Kitchen Sink   *Stink*
An example that may be distinctly apt.

Knife & Fork   *Pork*
A fairly well known term for what is known in backslang as 'kayrop'.

Knobbly Knee(s)   *Key(s)*
Asking if anyone has seen your 'knobbly knees' usually prompts a rude reply.

Knocker & Knob   *Job*
May be accessories to the door of opportunity, which during the recession of 1991 was slammed in millions of faces.

Knock on the Door   *Four*

Another example of bingo caller's slang. A 'knock' is seldom employed for £4 because the ever popular 'rofe', which is four in backslang, has been in vogue for many a year especially at the race track. *See* FRENCH LOAF.

Knotty Ash *Cash*

A modern piece inspired by the clash between the comedian Ken Dodd and the Inland Revenue. The inference being that the chief Diddy man's home in Knotty Ash contained money that was beyond the taxman's ken.

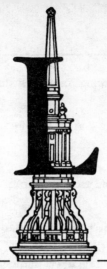

Lace Curtain   *Burton (Beer)*
Originally applied solely to this brand of beer but was later extended so that any type of ale became known as 'lace'.

La-Di-Da   *1 Car*
Coined when only the upper classes owned motorized transport.

2 Cigar
Generally condensed to a 'lardy' and once again symbolizes the social inequality of yesteryear, whereby the 'la-di-das' smoked cigars while the hoi polloi smoked cheap cigarettes.

Lady From Bristol   *Pistol*
'Stand and deliver,' said the highwayman as he cocked his 'lady from Bristol', as Dick Turpin's cockney biographer would have written.

Lady Godiva   *Fiver*
An old, but now barely used, term for £5. The backslang for which is a revif.

Lakes of Killarny   *1 Barmy*
Originally applied to idiocy but now in the reduced form of 'lakes' or 'lakie' it is more readily used as:

2 Carney
Refers to a two faced or 'double eyed' person, e.g., 'What a right lakie scrote him next door. Say's one thing to me

and something completely different to someone else.'

Lal Brough   *Snuff*
Commonly known as 'lally' when snuff was commonly used.

Lambeth Walk   *Chalk*
An example used by snooker and pool players.

Last Card in the Pack   *1 Sack*
To draw the 'last card' is to be dismissed from employment.

2 Snack
Refers to a bite to eat in the theatrical world.

Laugh & Joke   *Smoke*
Applies to a smoke of any kind, be it a pipe, cigar, cigarette or one of those funny fags.

Laurel & Hardy   *Bacardi*
Named after the most famous comedy duo of all time and generally shortened to the first name in which case Mr Laurel often acquires new partners, most commonly HOLY SMOKE (qv), i.e., Laurel and Holy. Stan Laurel (1890–1950) and Oiver Hardy (1892–1957).

Leaky Bladder   *Ladder*
A particularly high one is more likely to put a strain on the bowel rather than the bladder, especially in the acrophobic.

Lean & Linger   *Finger*
One of a few terms making the same rhyme. *See* LONG & and WAIT &.

Lean & Lurch   *Church*
An ancient term for some of our most ancient buildings.

Left & Right   *Fight*
Apt in that it is indicative of punches thrown or boots put in.

Left in the Lurch   *Church*
An extremely old example formed on the words of a music hall song about someone being jilted at the altar.

Leg Before Wicket   *Ticket*
Always abbreviated to the initials it refers to the obvious and also in the sense of a task done correctly, e.g., 'Put it over there by the window. That's the lbw.'
     A mentally inadequate person is said be 'not all the lbw'.

Leg of Beef   *Thief*
A variant of TEA LEAF (qv) which can only be used in the singular. Probably based on the nursery rhyme denouncing Taffy the Welshman.

Leg of Mutton   *Button*
Often truncated to the first element for comic effect, e.g., 'Mum, my leg's come off, can you sew it back on for me?'

Lemonade   *Spade*
Refers to a black person and the suit in a deck of cards.

Lemon Squeezer   *Geezer*
Nearly always reduced to a 'lemon'.

Lemon & Lime   *Time*
Applies to the time of day and to what is in short supply when you're in a hurry.

Lemon Curd   *Bird*
The feathered type is secondary to a young lady, obviously one who's a bit tasty.

Lemon Squash   *Wash*
Applies to the cleansing process and is employed in the same manner as BOB SQUASH (qv).

Len Hutton   *Button*
Formed on the name of a former England cricket captain but now seems to have come to the end of its innings as has the great man (1916–1990).

Lenny the Lion   *Iron (Homosexual)*
This is an uncommon example of twice removed RS IRON HOOF (qv) has become so widely used in its reduced form that is has picked up a term of its own. Based on the name of a ventriloquist's dummy from the early days of

television.

Levy & Frank   *Wank (Masturbate)*
A very familiar piece, in the shortened form of 'Levy', for the pulling of the pudding. Formed on the name of an old company of restaurateurs.

Life & Death   *Breath*
Normally used in the case of a person whose oral hygiene leaves something to be desired, i.e., 'dodgy life'. Suitable in that when people finally run out of breath they run out of life.

Liffey Water   *Porter*
Originally applied exclusively to this type of beer but was later expanded to refer to all kinds of the brown food, most frequently Guinness, which of course is black food.

Light & Dark   *Park*
Coined in the days when a family day out often constituted a day in the park, arriving in the morning and leaving when they were turfed out by the parkie with the advent of dusk.

Light of My Life   *Wife*
Often said sarcastically of a battle-axe.

Lillian Gish   *Fish*
Formed on the name of an American film actress who looked nothing like a fish. Whether or not she drank like one I don't know but this only applies to the creature as served on a platter.

Lilley & Skinner   *Dinner*
Named after the shoemaking company this is a well known term for the main repast of the day.

Limehouse Cut   *Gut*
Named after an east London waterway and refers to a paunch, e.g., 'Look at the massive Limehouse you're getting, you ought to go on a diet.'

Lincoln's Inn   *1 Fin*
Refers to a hand for which fin is an archaic piece of

slang.

2 Finn
A finn is an old racing term for £5. From finnuf, which is Yiddish for five.

3 Gin
A turn of the century piece that has been pushed aside by its more contemporary rivals.

Linen Draper   *Paper*
Specifically relates to a newspaper and is always folded to a 'linen'.

Lionel Blair   *Chair*
A fairly recent example from the world of showbiz formed on the name of a British dancer. A partner for BETTY GRABLE (qv)?

Lionel Blairs   *Flares*
A more recent variant of GROSVENOR SQUARES (qv) which enjoys wider employment.

Lion's Lair   *Chair*
A probably allusion to the 'old man's' chair that nobody else may sit in while he's in.

Lions Roar(ing)   *Snore/Snoring*
A totally apposite piece especially in relation to the Sunday afternoon drunk who annoying falls asleep in the armchair and snores his way through the film on the telly. Much to the consternation of the rest of the family who take turns to kick him and pinch his nose.

Lion's Share   *Chair*
A corruption of LION'S LAIR (qv).

Little & Large   *Marge*
A reference to the butter substitute, margarine.

Little Boy Blue   *Screw (Prison Officer)*
A piece that would appear to fit the bill perfectly.

Little Brown Jug   *Plug*
This old song title lends itself to an electric plug or the one in the sink. More vulgarly, though, to a tampon.

Little Miss Muffet *Stuff It*

An indication of what can be done with something that isn't welcome, e.g., 'You can take your advice and little Miss Muffet up your gongapooch.'

Little Nell *Bell*

Mainly applies to a door bell and is based on a character in an old melodrama.

Little Peter *Meter*

A gas or electric meter that has to be fed with money that is often the target for burglars. The term fits the word exactly, a meter being a small 'money box' and a Peter being a large one, i.e., a safe.

Little Tich(y) *Itch(y)*

Based on the name of a dwarf music hall comedian and is generally employed in the mosquito season. Tich was born Harry Relph in 1868 at the time of an infamous court case about the claim of a stranger to be the heir to the Tichbourne family fortune. The nickname stayed with him until his death in 1928 and it is due to him that short people will always be called 'Tich'.

Loaf of Bread *Head*

Most commonly used in relation to the internal workings of the noddle, hence the ultra familiar, 'use your loaf' as a directive to think.

Lollipop *1 Drop*

This is drop in the form of a gratuity, therefore to give anyone a 'lolly' is to give them a tip. This has evolved and entered the English language as a byword for money.

2 Shop

To 'lollipop' or 'lolly' is to inform on. Occasionally used to describe a shop.

Lollipop(s) *Cop(s)*

An infrequent reference to the police.

Londonderry *Sherry*

An elderly but rarely used piece.

London Fog *Dog*

An uncommon alternative to the regularly employed CHERRY HOG (qv).

London Taxi   *Jaxie (Anus)*
Often used when making a threat which may or may not be serious, e.g., 'If you don't leave off you'll get my boot six lace-holes up your London taxi.'

Lone Ranger   *Danger*
Never used in a sense of peril but as a term of exasperation, e.g., 'Any Lone Ranger of you ever paying me back the dough you owe me?'

Long Acre   *Baker*
An old example that is named after a historic London street that has been associated with Cromwell, Pepys, Dickens, Chippendale, various lords and ladies and John Logie Baird. But no Masters of the rolls (bakers).

Long(s) & Linger(s)   *Finger(s)*
Anatomically similar to WAIT & LINGER (qv).

Long & Short   *Port (Wine)*
The drink that may be long with a mixer or short on its own.

Loop the Loop   *Soup*
An old example that is spoken as 'loop de loop'.

Lord Lovat   *Shove It*
Employed in the same way as LITTLE MISS MUFFET (qv) and pronounced 'Lord love it'. Named after a World War Two brigadier of the Commandos.

Lord Lovel   *Shovel*
A navvy's term from the 19th century.

Lord Mayor   *Swear*
A very common reference to bad language that may be extended to 'Lord Mayoring'.

Lord of the Manor   *Tanner*
Refers to the old sixpence which survived decimalization for a while in the guise of 2½p. Up until the coin's demise this was one of the oldest terms of RS still in use and was

known as a 'lord'. Included for old time's sake.

Lord Sutch

1 Clutch
Based on the rock singing monster raving loony person who may never get to be an MP but is immortalized in rhyming slang which is much more prestigious. Applies, by the way, to what the motorist's left foot is for.

2 Crotch
Ill fitting trousers may be said to be a bit tight round the 'Screamin' Lord Sutch'.

Lord Wigg

Pig
Applies to a glutton or a discourteous person, e.g., 'Excuse my Lord Wigg, he's a friend.'

Lorna Doone

Spoon
Only in the rhyming slang can the beautiful heroine of a romantic novel end up in a bowl of spotted dick and custard.

Lost & Found

Pound
A very rare reference to £1.

Lousy Lou

Flu
I have no idea who the Lou in question was but he or she must be getting on a bit because this is a pretty old piece.

Love & Hate

Weight
This is associated with the constant battle between the human being and the scales, wherein we love to eat but hate to be fat.

Love & Kisses

Missus
A crawler's reference to his wife.

Love & Marriage

Carriage
A probable allusion to the horse drawn conveyance used at a traditional wedding.

Lover's Tiff

Syph (Syphilis)
In spite of the rhyme this is not restricted solely to this disease but to VD in general.

Lucky Dip(s) *Chip(s)*
Probably formed due to the fact that chips always taste best when eaten from a bag.

Lucozade *Spade*
Another derogatory reference to a black person.

Lucy Locket *Pocket*
Refers to where one's hands seem to belong, often to the annoyance of a foreman from whom, 'Take your bleeding hands out of your Lucy Lockets and do some work' is common rucking.

Luger Lout *Kraut*
A World War Two German as described by a wag watching *The Great Escape*.

Lump of Coke *Bloke*
Large gentlemen are often spoken of as 'big lumps'.

Lump of Ice *Advice*
Often needed when you're in hot water.

Lump of Lead *Head*
Can be used to describe a weighty bonce after a heavy night.

Lump of School *Fool*
Ancient term that may be familiar when reduced to the first element, e.g., 'You stupid great lump.'

Lumpy Gravy *Navy*
The Royal Navy as named by members of the other services.

Marcaroni — *Pony*
This is a long established term for £25. It is also a piece of twice removed RS referring to excrement. The reduced form of PONY & TRAP (qv) has become a by-word for crap and is now commonly known as 'maca'.

Macaroon — *Coon*
An oft used example that does nothing to harbour good race relations.

Mac Gimp — *Pimp*
The prostitute's bully, known as a 'mac'.

Madam De Luce — *Spruce (Deceive)*
Extensively employed in the first element, a conman may try to 'madam' you by giving you a 'load of old madam'.

Mae West — *Chest*
Named after the American film star, who was the sex symbol of her day, this is anatomically exclusive to the female chest. It applies internally, where pains may occur as well as externally whereby the term is similarly employed for *Breast*. Ms West (1892–1980) is remembered as much for her quotations as for her films.

Magistrate's Court — *Short*
A drinker's reference to a short measure or spirit, e.g., 'a drop of magistrate's'. Which is appropriate since it is where a lot of people end up as a result of too many.

Mahatma Gandhi   *Shandy*
Not often used by Cockneys who tend to have difficulty getting their tongues round the first element. It either comes out as Me'atma or Meratma. It has also been used in relation to brandy but since the man was a tee-totaller this would appear to be more suitable. Born in 1869 the leader of the home rule for India movement was assassinated in 1948.

Major Stevens   *Evens*
The only time evens can be odds is in the racing game.

Man Alive   *Five*
A piece of bingo caller's jargon. Is also occasionally a reference to £5.

Man & Wife   *Knife*
Often used to describe a pen-knife or that of a workman.

Manchester City   *Titty*
A rare alternative to the oft quoted BRISTOL CITY (qv).

Mangle & Wring(er) *Sing(er)*
Normally used in association with a singer of no great vocal talent, like the person who regularly takes the stage at the local and 'mangles' 'My Way'.

Manhole Cover   *Brother*
A piece used mainly in the third person and stunted to 'manhole'.

Man in the Moon   *Loon*
A reference to an eccentric.

Man o' War   *Bore*
Apt when applied to the man who trots out tales of heroism in the western desert etc *ad infinitum*.

Marble Halls   *Balls (Testicles)*
Always shortened to marbles.

Marbles & Conkers *Bonkers (Mad)*
A juvenile term based on two games of childhood that is always reduced to the first element. Apt in as much as

adults who continue to play these games and enter championships are considered thus by pseudo sophisticates who would secretly love to do the same thing.

Margate Sand(s) *Hand(s)*
An alternative to neighbouring RAMSGATE SAND(S) (qv).

Maria Monk *Spunk (Semen)*
A very old example that is based on a dirty book of the 19th century.

Marie Corelli *Telly*
A term that goes back to the early days of television, named after a long departed romantic novelist.

Mars & Venus *Penis*
Used jokingly and referred to as a 'Mars bar'.

Martin-Le-Grand *Hand*
A very old piece based on a London street (St Martins-le-Grand).

Marty Wilde *Mild (Ale)*
Had a slight currency when the man was making hit records and the beer was still popular.

Mary Ann *Fan*
Applies to a cooler, either electric or hand held.

Mary Ellens *Melons (Breasts)*
A contemporary term for what is a fairly modern piece of slang.

Mary Green *Queen*
In short 'the Mary', which only applies to the playing card.

Marylou *Glue*
A lady not to be sniffed at.

Maud & Ruth *Truth*
An example from the pens of television scriptwriters.

Max Factor *Actor*
Not necessarily he who treads the boards but a person

who feigns injury, illness or innocence to gain advantage, the Italian footballer is a classic example. Based on the cosmetics company which would appear to be most apposite.

Max Miller   *Pillow*
Based on the great English comedian who, according to his act, pillowed every barmaid in Brighton. Known as the 'Cheekie Chappie' Max is reckoned to be the guv'nor of stand-up comedy (1895–1963).

Max Walls   *Balls (Testicles)*
Often shortened to 'Maxies' after the late English comic who shares the bill with KEN DODDS (qv). Although considered by many to have been a genius of comedy, towards the end of his life Max Wall (1908–90) proved to be a fine serious actor. In backslang 'balls' turn into 'slabs'.

Maxwell House   *Mouse*
Modern and based on a brand of coffee.

Mazawatee   *Potty*
Formed on the name of a brand of tea in reference to anyone who is two ounces short of a pound.

Me & You   *Menu*
A piece long thought of as being RS but would appear to be more of a play on words.

Meat & Two Veg   *Reg*
The diminutive of Reginald is 'Meat'.

Meat Pie   *Fly*
Apart from being an unsavoury reference to the insect, it also applies to what should be adjusted before leaving.

Mechanical Digger   *Nigger*
A derogatory term that is reduced to the first element. It is probably an allusion to the legendary capacity for hard work ascribed to the black person.

Melvin Bragg   *Shag (Coitus)*
Based on the name of a television celebrity and author, this is the newest term in the book. In 1992, a serial, writ-

ten by Mr Bragg, was shown on British TV. The production contained many sex scenes and as a consequence the act of lovemaking immediately became known as a 'Melvin'.

Merchant Banker   *Wanker*
An 80s piece for a contemptible person coined by young East Enders in reference to the yuppie types who moved on to their 'patch' around that time.

Merlin the   *Pigeon*
Magician   Always known as a 'Merlin' because of number of syllables involved.

Merry & Bright(s)   *Light(s)*
Fittingly applies to illumination.

Merry Go Round   *Pound*
A 'Merry' is £1.

Merry Old Soul   *1 Coal*
Common when coal fires were prevalent. *See* JEREMIAH.

2 Hole
Applies to any orifice including the anus.

Michael Caine   *Pain*
Whereby a pest may be a 'Michael in the Khyber'. Named after the London born actor who has achieved fame and fortune by being a professional cockney.

Micky Bliss   *Piss*
Seldom used in association with urination but in the sense of 'taking the piss' meaning to deride or insult. Taking the 'micky' is supremely common in this guise, transcending the world of RS. Sometimes extended to 'extracting the Michael'.

Mickey Mouse   *1 House*
Probably the commonest piece for the two up, two down at this time. Based on the giant rodent of Disneyland.

2 Scouse
A contemporary example used mockingly by London football supporters against their Merseyside rivals. The derision stems from the non-rhyming slang meaning of

the term which is second rate or inferior.

Mickey Rooney   *Loony*
Named (some would say aptly) after the multi-divorced Hollywood actor, in regard to a person otherwise known as 'nut rock'.

Micro Chip   *Nip (Japanese)*
Shortened to 'micro' this is as recent as it is appropriate since they lead the world in this technology. It is also indicative of the widespread perception of the size of the average son of Nippon.

Mike Malone   *Phone*
Sounds like this is based on a tough guy but he can't get the better of the DOG (qv).

Mile End   *Friend*
Mostly employed in an introductory sense, e.g., 'I'd like you to meet a Mile End of mine.' Based on a well known area of east London.

Mince Pie(s)   *Eye(s)*
Very well known and always known as 'mince' or 'minces'.

Milkman's Horse   *Cross (Angry)*
A dated and probably extinct animal that was normally employed when warning a child against acting up.

Misbehave   *Shave*
When a man says that he is going into the bathroom to misbehave you now know what he is doing. Or do you?

Mix & Muddle   *Cuddle*
One of life's great annoyances is when you're lying in bed on a cold night, having a nice 'mix & muddle' and you have to get up to have a CUDDLE & KISS (qv).

Moby Dick   *1 Nick*
The 'Moby' is a rare reference to prison.

2 Sick
Time away from work due to illness is known as being 'on the Moby Dick'. Also an obvious reference to venereal

disease, e.g., Q. Moby Dick? A. It certainly is!

Mods & Rockers *Knockers (Bosoms)*
Based on a couple of youth cultures of the 60s, this applies to breasts of the fuller variety, the type which have caused men to wax lyrical down the ages. 'Cor, look at the mods on that,' is a phrase that springs to mind.

Mogadored *Floored*
This refers to being baffled or beaten by a problem. The assembly instructions to anything bought from a DIY shop induces much puzzled head scratching and the comment, 'I can't make head nor tail of this. I'm totally mogadored.'

Molly Malone *Phone*
The seafood seller from the fair city of Dublin is another telecommunications rival to, and mostly seen off by, the 'dog'. *See* DOG & BONE.

Molly O'Morgan *Organ*
Originally referred to a barrel organ but later to any organ not necessarily musical.

Mona Lisa *Freezer*
Where else but in RS can a great work of art be mentioned in the same breath as a fish finger.

Monkey's Tail(s) *Nail(s)*
A carpenter's term for this type of hardware.

Moody & Sankey *Hanky Panky (Deception)*
Something that isn't quite what it seems is often referred to as 'moody'. The week off work with a 'moody' backache isn't the truth and a conman will give you a load of old 'moody'. The term is so common that it has acquired a piece of RS of it's own. *See* PUNCH & JUDY.

Montezumas *Bloomers*
Applies to that type of underwear that is now mainly seen on a seaside postcard.

Mop & Bucket *Fuck It*
The thing to shout if you hit your thumb with a hammer. If such restraint is possible.

More or Less **Dress**
Applies to a garment rather than the act of getting dressed. Probably based on the shifting hemlines and necklines of fashion.

Moriarty **Party**
Often decreased to a 'Mori' and named after the arch enemy of Sherlock Holmes and Neddy Seagoon.

Morning Glory **Cory (Penis)**
Would appear to refer to one that is 'piss proud' on waking.

Morris Minor **Shiner (Black Eye)**
Based on a make of car which needn't necessarily have a smashed headlamp.

Mortar & Trowel **Towel**
An ancient piece not often heard outside the washroom of a building site.

Mother & Daughter **1 Water**
An archaic term for the wet element.

2 Quarter
A riverman's piece for a riverside post used for tying up boats.

Mother Brown **Town**
Sometimes used in connection with the West End of London.

Mother Hubbard **Cupboard**
An obvious piece from the world of nursery rhymes.

Mother-in-Law **Saw**
A chippy's term for the main tool of his trade.

Mother Kelly **1 Jelly**
Applies obviously to the sweet and to the eels' accompaniment but is also employed in connection with abject fear, e.g., 'This vicious looking dog came bounding towards me barking its head off. Well, my legs turned to Mother Kelly.'

2 Telly

A more recent development than (1). Based on the lady with the famous doorstep.

Mother of Mine   *Nine*
A term once used by bingo callers. Rarely used in reference to £9.

Mother of Pearl   *Girl*
Normally preceded by 'the old' or 'my old' and meaning the wife. A lot of older cockney's refer to their better halves as 'mother' or 'mum'.

Mother's Pride   *Bride*
An apposite term for the radiant star of the wedding.

Mother's Ruin   *Gin*
An early and very familiar example which is symbolic of what was traditionally a woman's drink. Not a great rhyme but apt in a lot of cases.

Moulin Rouge   *Stooge*
A theatrical term for a comedian's foil.

Mountain Passes   *Glasses*
Scenic routes for spectacular viewing.

Mountains of Mourne   *Horn (Erection)*
Probably inspired by appearances above the sheets due to stirrings beneath.

Mouse Trap   *Nap*
Refers to forty winks. Or in Nelson's case twenty.

Mouthwash   *Nosh*
A very appropriate piece since nosh is a slang term for fellatio.

Mozart & Lizt   *Pissed (Drunk)*
A piece that was composed in the theatre and performed on radio and television before gaining a wider usage. *See* BRAHMS & LISZT.

Mozzle and Brocha   *Knocker*
The knocker in question is a door knocker, to be on which is the trade of the door-to-door salesman. This was

the original meaning of the term but to be 'on the mozzle' now lends itself to borrowing, a neighbour for instance may be on it for a cup of sugar.

Mr Hyde

Snide
A variant of JEKYLL & HYDE (qv) but this is more likely to refer to a person than an object, e.g., 'Don't trust him, he's a right Mr Hyde.'

Mrs Chant

Aunt
This bears no relation to the relative but to the toilet, for which 'aunt' is a polite euphemism. This appears to be one in the eye for Mrs Ormiston Chant who was the Mary Whitehouse of the music hall era.

Mrs Duckett

1 Bucket
A piece that was common in the fishmonger trade and has been employed in the building industry.

2 Fuck It!
If a workman had a mishap at a place where swearing would be considered unseemly, 'Mrs Duckett' would have to suffice. But said with the right volume and intonation it does give a certain amount of satisfaction.

Mrs Mopp

Shop
The place to do the 'Mrs Mopping'. Named after a character from the old radio show ITMA.

Mrs More

Floor
One can walk on, sit on and, when drunk, fall on 'the Mrs'. From the song 'Don't have any more Mrs More'.

Muddy Trench

French
Possibly a rhyme on 'bloody French', which is how most Englishmen view 'them over there'. Although it will never replace 'frog'.

Muffin Baker

Quaker
This is an extremely old piece which basically means to be constipated. A Quaker is the name given to excrement that is 'baked hard' thus causing a bridger.

Mum & Dad

Mad
Another reference to those with their 'boots on the

wrong feet'.

Mumble & Mutter *Butter*
Shortened to 'mumble' and spread on your UNCLE FRED (qv).

Mustard Pot *Twat (Vagina)*
That of a passionately hot lady.

Mutt & Jeff *Deaf*
Based on a couple of comic strip characters, this is a very well known example and is most commonly reduced to 'Mutton'.

Mutton Pie *Eye*
In reference to eyes, this is definitely in the shadow of MINCE PIE but a person with an eye defect or a wayward eye is often called 'Mutton' eye.

Myrna Loy *Saveloy*
Not a great rhyme but quite widely used. Named after a Hollywood actress.

My Word *Turd*
Just the right exclamation when you slip on one, crack your head on the pavement and get dog's mess all over your best suit. I should cocoa!

Nancy Lee

1 Flea
This was fairly common when fleas were.

2 Tea
Not as well known as sister ROSIE (qv).

Nanny Goat

1 Boat
An old piece that has sunk without trace due to the popularity of:

2 Throat
A common cause of a day off work is a sore 'nanny'.

3 Tote
Possibly the widest usage of the term is used in racing circles for the totalisator.

Nantucket

Bucket
Had a limited employment on a building site in the 70s.

National Debt

Bet
A reference to gambling that would be more appropriate if it were 'personal debt'. But it aint!

National Front

Cunt
Modern term for an obnoxious person based on the right wing political movement.

National Hunt

Front
Employed in the same fashion as JAMES HUNT (qv) and used as 'having more National Hunt than Cheltenham'.

Nat King Cole

1 Dole
A piece from the late 50s that was an update of OLD KING COLE (qv).

2 Mole
A reference to a growth on the skin (naevus).

3 Roll
Applies to a bread roll. Based on the well known singer/pianist (1919–65).

Naughton & Gold

Cold
Refers to the physical condition of having a cold. Named after a British double act that was part of the Crazy Gang, Charlie Naughton (1887–1976) and Jimmy Gold (1886–1967).

Nautical Miles

Piles
Normally shrunk to 'nauticals', this is another reference to a complaint that non-sufferers find amusing.

Navigator

Potato
An archaic term for the earth apple, once gainfully employed in the cry of itinerant baked potato vendors, whereby NAVIGATOR SCOT served as potato hot.

Near & Far

Bar
Refers to a bar room, either public or saloon, rather than the actual timber (counter).

Ned Kelly

1 Belly
Based on the name of a 19th century Australian outlaw, the term is trying to steal the thunder of the long standing DERBY KELLY (qv).

2 Telly
Modern and possibly formed after a film of his exploits appeared on it. Kelly was born in 1855 and hanged in 1880.

Needle & Cotton

Rotten
Can apply to anything that is less than pleasant, from a maggot-ridden apple to a nasty person. May also be said of the person's insides after eating the apple.

Needle & Pin

1 Gin

An old piece that is usually crashed down to a 'drop of needle'.

2 Thin
Would appear to be a particularly relevant example.

Needle & Thread — *Bread*
Often used in conjunction with STAMMER & STUTTER (qv) to form a convoluted piece. 'A slice of needle and stammer' (bread and butter) would be impossible for the uninitiated to fathom out.

Nell Gwyn — *Gin*
The mistress of Charles II lends her name to the spirit of the East End. An actress, born in 1650, she bore the king two sons before dying in 1687.

Nellie Bligh — *Fly*
Applies to the flying pest of summer. Based on the name of the other woman in the song 'Frankie and Johnny'.

Nellie Dean — *Queen*
A reference to a homosexual male especially an older one, e.g., 'an old Nellie'. Named after the eponymous heroine of a music hall song.

Nellie Dean(s) — *Green(s)*
Green vegetables are normally boiled down to the Christian name as is a green snooker ball.

Nellie Duff — *Puff (Breath)*
Through breath we get life hence the well known phrase, 'not on your Nellie', meaning 'not on your life'.

Nelson Eddy(s) — *Ready(s)*
Can be used impatiently whilst waiting for somebody, e.g., 'Aint you Nelson Eddy yet?' But is chiefly employed in connection with cash, e.g., 'If you've got the Nelsons you can take it away now.' Formed on the name of an American musical actor (1901–67).

Nelson Riddle — *Fiddle*
Named after an American musician and composer but has nothing to do with music. People who make a living on the very edge of legality are said to have 'a few Nelson

Riddles going'.

Nervo & Knox

1 Box
Mainly applies to the 'goggle box', i.e., the television and is generally known as 'the Nervo'. Formed on the comedy pairing who were part of the Crazy Gang; Jimmy Nervo (1890–1975) and Teddy Knox (1896–1974).

2 Pox (VD)
Often truncated to the name of the first partner.

Never Fear

Beer
A very old piece perhaps based on the bravado that may come from having one bevvypint over the eight.

Never Again

Ben (Truman)
A term, for a brand of beer, that is based on what every hungover person has said. Hundreds of times.

New Delhi

Belly
An appropriate example for the rumbling one following a particularly powerful curry.

Newgate Jail

Tale
Archaic term for a hard luck story.

Newington Butts

Guts
Formed on the name of a south London street this may be used anatomically, e.g., a pain or a punch in the 'Newingtons' or to courage, e.g., the 'Newingtons' to stand up for yourself.

Niagara Falls

1 Balls (Testicles)
The 'Niagaras' for short.

2 Stalls
A theatrical reference to that part of a theatre.

Nice Enough

Puff (Homosexual)
Widely known as 'one of those nice boys'.

Nice One Cyril

Squirrel
Based on a catch phrase of the early 70s that got ridiculously popular. Started by supporters of Tottenham Hotspur FC and directed at their full back Cyril Knowles, it was taken up and used in an advertising campaign for a

brand of bread. It soon spread nationwide and it seemed like everyone was saying it. In 1973 a song of that name even got into the charts. Of late it has become more and more common to see squirrels in parks and gardens in and around London hence this modernish piece of RS which is usually shortened to a 'nice one'.

Nicker Bits   *Shits*
An example that proves the continuing coinage of terms of RS. The pound coin was introduced in 1983 and was immediately nicked-named a nicker bit. This piece for diarrhoea followed shortly afterwards.

Night & Day   *1 Grey*
A reference to the ageing process as seen in the colour of a mature head of hair. A worried mother may tell a troublesome offspring 'You'll have me night and day before my time.'

2 Play
A theatrical performance.

Nig Nog   *Wog*
An abusive term mainly used against black people although it originally referred to all foreigners irrespective of colour.

Nits & Lice(s)   *Price(s)*
An early example coined by those laying the odds, the bookmakers.

Noah's Ark   *1 Dark*
Cricketers have to up-stumps when it gets too 'Noah's ark'.

2 Nark (Informer)
An old term which Spoonerizes very cleverly. Oah's (whore's) nark represents extreme despicability.

Nobby Halls   *Balls (Testicles)*
Based on the eponymous hero of a comic song who 'only had one ball'.

Nobby Stiles   *Piles*
Named after the hard tackling member of England's victorious world cup team of 1966 who was a constant pain

in the arse of opponents. The 'Nobbies' for short.

North & South   *Mouth*
A very famous piece immortalized in the song 'What a mouth'.

North Pole   *Hole (Anus)*
An old example that has lost out to SOUTH POLE (qv) which has the edge in directional relevance.

Nose & Chin   *Win*
Not uncommon when gambling to have a bet 'on the nose' meaning money has been placed on a horse or dog to win.

Noser My Knacker   *Tobacco*
Reduced to 'noser' the term literally means 'smell my testicles' which is an old cockney reply to an admonishment. This has now been replaced by a one word answer beginning with B having more or less the same meaning. This extinct piece is said to have originated in the late 19th century with a smoker's retaliation to complaints from non-smokers.

Nutmeg(s)   *Leg(s)*
A piece of footballer's jargon whereby to play the ball through an opponent's legs is to 'nutmeg' him.

Oak & Ash   *Cash*
A term emanating from the theatre, possibly a connection between out of work actors and wood.

Oats & Barley   *Charlie*
One of a small number of Christian names to be endowed with a piece of RS. It also serves in reference to a fool, in which case it becomes a piece of slang for slang. *See* CHARLIE HUNT.

Oats & Chaff   *Path*
An archaic reference to a footpath that is now worn out.

Obadiah   *Fire*
A piece to rival that other biblical gentleman JEREMIAH (qv).

Ocean Liner   *Shiner (Black Eye)*
Normally decreased to the first element in relation to what was known as 'half a surprise'. This was due to the words of the well known song 'Two lovely black eyes, oh what a surprise'.

Ocean Wave   *Shave*
One of several terms for destubblizing the 'boat'. *See* BOAT RACE.

Oedipus Rex   *Sex*
Doesn't sound particularly wholesome since it is based on the name of a man who married his mother.

Office Worker   *Shirker*

A long held view by manual workers is that their pen pushing counterparts do not work very hard. Office wallahs are often referred to as 'lightenders' or the 'shiny bum brigade' and labourers find the phrase 'a hard day at the office' amusing, and scornfully retort, 'Call that bloody work?' Therefore anybody not pulling his weight is called an 'office worker'.

Oh My Dear   *Beer*

'A pint of oh' is an ancient bar order now obsolete.

Oh My God   *Bald*

God in cockney dialect is always pronounced 'Gawd' so the rhyme is better than it looks. A long lost associate who's hair loss is apparent may be greeted with the words, 'Oh my Gawd he's gone oh my Gawd.' Extreme baldness is sometimes extended to 'Oh my GOOD Gawd'.

Oil Slick   *Spick*

Formed in the early days of the package holiday to the Costas, when young Spanish males typically used masses of hair cream and tried to use their Latin smarm to pull female tourists.

Oil Tanker   *Wanker*

An abusive term directed at the obnoxious or the useless. Often the pilot of one of these oversized vessels who, through rank bad navigation, has caused colossal devastation to the environment.

Oily Rag   *Fag*

An old example but one which still has a lot of puff left in it.

Okey Doke   *Poke*

Condensed to 'okey' this refers to a wallet or more specifically to what it contains. A low-life term of the pickpocket.

Old Bag   *Hag*

In its original form this applied to an old or infected prostitute who, presumably, wasn't cover girl material. It has since become supremely common in reference to any disagreeable woman.

Old Iron & Brass
1 Grass
An order from an over officious parkie is 'Keep off the old iron.'

2 Pass
A military term regarding what's needed to get out of barracks.

Old Jamaica Rum
Sun
Always decreased to the first two elements this old naval piece has probably sunk below the horizon.

Old King Cole
Dole
One of the older pieces regarding unemployment benefit.

Old Nag
Fag
A long since stubbed out piece that was first ignited by World War One Tommies.

Old Oak
Smoke
Refers to London, otherwise known as 'the smoke'.

Old Rag
Flag
A term used by all but the fiercely patriotic.

Old Whip
Ship
An early seaman's term for his own ship, that is the one he is currently serving on.

Oliver Twist
Fist
An ancient example that is always known by the Christian name of this Dickensian orphan.

Oliver Reed
Weed
Known as the 'dreaded Ollie' this is a reference to tobacco often used by holier than thou non-smokers. Named after the British actor this takes in all forms of tobacco including marijuana. More recently the term has been connected with another type of drug, namely *Speed* (Amphetamines).

Once A Week
1 Beak (Magistrate)

An example that was probably coined by a habitual reprobate.

2 Cheek
An allusion to non-edible sauce as may be poured on by a liberty taker and takes the form of a 'oncer'.

One & Eight   *Plate*
Takes in all kinds of plate including crockery, a forger's plate and the one passed around in church. Sometimes, but rarely, used as twice removed slang for feet, e.g., 'My one and eights are killing me.' *See* PLATES OF MEAT.

One & Half   *Scarf*
Either a headscarf or a choker.

One & T'other   *1 Brother*
A bit confusing really because this is also used for:

2 Mother
In either case it is always employed in full and in the third person.

One(s) & Two(s)   *Shoe(s)*
One gets one's 'ones' from one's personal 'ones' maker. As a cockney royal might say.

One for his Nob   *Bob*
A once common reference to a shilling (5p) often given as a tip in which case it symbolically still survives. The term is representative of something on top, coming as it does from the game of cribbage whereby to hold the jack of the upturned suit encrues an extra point.

On the Floor   *Poor*
A very common piece that has transcended the ranks of RS because of its total suitability. To be on the floor is to be as low as you can get.

Orange Pip   *Nip*
An 'orange' is an allusion to a person from Japan which, colour wise, would appear to be incorrect.

Orchestra Stalls   *Balls (Testicles)*
The 'orchestras' is another suggestion for the scrotal area.

Organ Grinder   *Minder*
A reference to a bodyguard that brings tears to the eyes.

Orinoko   *1 Cocoa*
The bedtime beverage sometimes called 'ori'.

2 Poker
Always cocknified to 'orinoker' for the fireside implement.

Oscar Asche   *Cash*
Always curtailed to 'Oscar', this is a time honoured piece, formed on the name of a long departed actor.

Oscar Wilde   *Mild (Ale)*
Not often heard now that this type of beer is all but obsolete in London. Although a northerner might say that all decent beer is obsolete in the capital. And he'd get no argument from me. After the Irish born novelist, playwright and outstanding wit (1854–1900) who courted controversy by courting Lord Alfred Douglas.

Ounce of Baccy   *Paki*
With the prevalence of the Asian tobacconist this term just had to happen. Often reduced to an 'ouncer'.

Overcoat Maker   *Undertaker*
An obvious allusion to a wooden overcoat.

Over the Stile   *Trial*
Employed as being 'sent over' or having to 'stand over the stile'. This is an ancient term.

Owen Nares   *Chairs*
Another example from theatre land based on the name of an actor (1888–1943) from the early days of cinema.

Oxford Scholar   *Dollar*
A dollar was five shillings in £.s.d and is still used by some die hards in regard to 25p. The term therefore still has a small currency.

Oxo Cube   *Tube*
This is the London underground system which is well known as 'the oxo'.

Paddy & Mick   *Thick (Stupid)*
Based on the names of the two typical Irishmen who have kept a host of comedians in business.

Pain in the Neck   *Cheque*
An example that may have been coined by the recipient of a bouncer.

Panoramas   *Pyjamas*
A piece that is mainly employed when getting children ready for bed.

Pants & Vest   *Best*
A drinker's reference to best bitter (ale), e.g., 'a pint of pants'.

Paper Bag   *Nag*
A reference to a tongue larruping, many a last pint has been refused because, 'I couldn't stand her papering me all night.'

Paper Doll   *Moll*
A moll is an old slang term for a harlot.

Partick Thistle   *Whistle*
The Scottish football team lends its name to both the noun and the verb.

Pat & Mike   *Bike*
Those two Irish lads in tandem again.

Pat Malone   *Alone*
To be on your 'Pat' is a less well known version of being on your 'Tod' or 'Jack' *See* TOD SLOANE and JACK JONES.

Peace & Quiet   *Diet*
Some people go on a 'peace and quiet' just to get a bit of peace of quiet from their spouses.

Pearly Gate   *Plate*
A dinner plate, often a part of the best service.

Pearly King   *Ring (Anus)*
The ring or ringpiece are old slang terms for this part of the anatomy. Hence the choice expression, 'Poke it up your pearly!'

Pease Pudding Hot   *Snot (Nasal Mucus)*
Always reduced to the first two elements, e.g., 'I need a clean hanky, this one's full of pease pudding.'

Pea-shooter   *Hooter*
A fairly old allusion to the nose that shouldn't be confused with PEE-shooter which is a different extremity altogether. The term is sometimes used in connection with a car horn.

Peas in the Pot   *Hot*
Always boiled down to 'peas', this applies to temperature and to a person's expertise or skill.

Peckham Rye   *Tie*
Ultra famous and always condensed to a 'Peckham' in reference to what supposedly creates a good impression when worn.

Pedigree Chum   *Come*
A term for the unromantic clod, this applies to both semen and orgasm.

Pedlar's Pack   *Sack (Dismissal)*
A modernish rival to the long established TIN TACK (qv).

Pen & Ink   *Stink*
Old and very common expression for a bad smell.

Pen & Inker   *Stinker*
A dated piece for a scoundrel or a particularly tough problem.

Penn'orth of Bread   *Head*
A stale reference to the hat peg.

Penn'orth of Chalk   *Walk*
Always dislengthened to the first element often when sending someone out of earshot, e.g., 'Take a penn'orth, I want to talk to your mother, private like.'

Penny a Mile   *Smile*
Always reduced to the first element, e.g., 'Come on, cheer up, give us a penny.'

Penny a Pound   *Ground*
Terra firma is known as the 'penny'.

Penny Banger   *Clanger (Mistake)*
Often used apologetically, e.g., 'Look, I'm sorry, I dropped a penny banger and it blew up in my face.'

Penny Black   *Back*
Employed only in an anatomical sense. More man-hours are lost through bad 'pennies' than anything else.

Penny Bun   *1 One*
Only really used in connection with odds whereby 'a cockle to a penny bun' is 10 to 1. *See* COCKEREL & HEN.

2 Son 3 Sun
One of several examples emanating from the baker's shop making the same rhyming connection.

Peppermint Rocks   *Socks*
Not too familiar due to the popularity of ALMOND ROCKS (qv).

Percy Thrower   *Blower*
A fairly modern piece for what is an old slang term for a telephone. Named after the celebrated gardening expert.

Perry Como   *Homo*

An outdated example for an old fashioned term for a homosexual male. Based on the name of an American singer for no other reason than its rhyming factor.

Peter Pan *Van*
A youthful piece that seems to be restricted to the light haulage industry.

Petticoat Lane *Pain*
Can either be used in connection with physical pain or to a nuisance (a pain in the neck). Called after the famous Sunday market at Aldgate E1.

PG Tips *Lips*
The larger types presumably, as brandished by the chimpanzees in the famous adverts for this brand of tea. Generally known as 'pee gees'.

Ps & Qs *Shoes*
In normal speech to mind your Ps and Qs is to be careful of what you say and do and not 'put your foot in it'. In RS, however, if you don't put your foot in your P & Q it's not worth having it.

Pheasant Plucker *Fucker*
Not absolutely sure that this famous Spoonerism can be admissible as RS. It is used in the same context as, 'He's a nice bastard' meaning the opposite. A 'pheasant plucker', therefore, is not a nice person.

Philharmonic *Tonic (Water)*
The perfect accompaniment for VERA LYNN (qv).

Phil the Fluter *Shooter (Gun)*
Known as a 'Phil' and named after the Irish musician with the celebrated ball.

Photo Finish *Guinness*
The well known stout is often downed to a 'photer'.

Piccadilly *Silly*
Normally reduced to the first two syllables, e.g., 'Don't be so picca.'

Piccolo & Flute *Suit*

A rare version of the well worn WHISTLE & FLUTE (qv).

Pick & Choose   *Booze*
To be 'on the pick' is an alternative to being 'on the river'. *See* RIVER OUSE.

Pick up Sticks   *Six*
An example from an old game of bingo.

Pie & Liquor   *Vicar*
Normally decreased to the first element with 'the old' as a prefix. The liquor of the piece is the gravy served in the pie and mash shops.

Pie & Mash   *1 Cash*
In the cab and courier industry a 'pie and mash job' is a fare or job that is not on account.

2 Slash
Very common for those whose 'back teeth are floating', i.e., possessed of a painfully full bladder, to disappear behind whatever cover is available for a 'pie & mash'. Based on a traditional London dish.

Pie & One   *1 Son*
Based on the same fare as in the previous entry, i.e., pie and one portion of mashed potato.

2 Sun
Where presumably it becomes 'pie' in the sky.

Pieces of Eight   *Weight*
The aim of the dieter is to 'do some pieces'.

Pig & Roast   *Toast*
A term coined by soldiers in the 'second lot' that didn't survive the peace.

Piggy Bank   *Wank (Masturbate)*
Normally rubbed down to the first element.

Pig in the Middle   *Piddle*
Either used in full or condensed to a 'pig' but never a 'piggy'. An announcement of 'I'm going for a quick piggy' means something completely different. *See previous item.*

Pig's Ear   *Beer*
The most famous term for what has rapidly become an expensive hobby.

Pig's Fry   *Tie*
A seldom used alternative to the widely used PECKHAM RYE (qv).

Pillar & Post   *Ghost*
Whereby the holy trinity becomes 'the soap, currant and holy pillar and post'.

Pimple & Blotch   *Scotch*
Commonly abridged to a 'drop of pimple'.

Pimple & Wart   *Port (Wine)*
Used in full so as to avoid confusion with the previous entry.

Pin(s) & Needle(s)   *Beetle(s)*
These insects have always been pronounced 'beedles'.

Pineapple Chunk   *Bunk*
Apart from referring to a bed, to 'do a pineapple' is to abscond.

Pink Lint   *Skint*
An infrequent interloper into the popularity of BORACIC LINT (qv) as an expression of having 'nuppence' in your pocket.

Pinky & Perky   *Turkey*
A modernish piece for what is traditionally eaten on festive occasions. Although based on the names of a brace of TV puppets who happened to be pigs, a slice of 'Pinky' is not a slice of pork.

Pipe & Drum   *Bum*
In contrast to FIFE & DRUM (qv) this applies to the anus whereby 'poke it up your pipe' is a common synonym for 'stick it where the sun don't shine'.

Pipe Your Eye   *Cry*
Debatable whether this is genuine RS or not but it has been given as an example for a long time so it warrants

inclusion. Children have been told to 'stop piping' and excited people have been ordered to 'pipe down' for generations.

Piss Pot   *Sot (Drunkard)*
Could the word 'pissed' meaning drunk stem from here? It would appear to be relevant due to the amount of times an inebriate would have used this receptacle during the night.

Pitch & Fill   *Bill*
Originally an RS term for the Christian name which later applied to a poster.

Pitch & Toss   *Boss*
A reference to him or her in charge.

Plain & Gravy   *Navy*
Referred to as the 'plain' and based on that culinary delight the dumpling and gravy.

Plate of Beef   *Chief*
An allusion to a chief warder, otherwise known as a 'screwdriver'.

Plate of Ham   *Gam (Fellatio)*
Always reduced to the first element and is supremely common whereby 'to plate' becomes a verb. Many a filthy comment was raised in the early days of betting shops when it was announced over the blower that a race was delayed because a horse was being plated. 'It's a good job jockey's are little, it saves getting their knees dirty', is one I seem to remember. Gam is an abbreviation of gameroosh which seems to be a corruption of an old French word for the performance of oral sex, gamahucher.

Plates & Dishes   *Missus*
'The plates' is an old reference to the wife.

Plates of Meat   *Feet*
The fame of this term is legendary and the leg ends are always known as 'plates'.

Platters of Meat   *Feet*

A rarely used variant of the previous item, except, maybe, in matters of the patter of tiny 'platters'.

Pleasure & Pain　　*Rain*
Apt since the umbrella maker's pleasure is the holiday maker's pain.

Plink Plonk　　*Vin Blanc*
A term coined on the battlefields of World War One. Plonk was soldier's jargon for mud which was likened to the cheap wines available. A result of which, 'plonk' has become a common hand-me-down for all dodgy wine.

Plymouth Argyll　　*File*
A modernish alternative to DUKE OF ARGYLL (qv).

Plymouth Cloak　　*Oak*
An archaic piece for an even older slang term for a cosh.

Polish & Gloss　　*Toss (Masturbate)*
Generally shortened to 'polish' or 'polish off'. *See* GRANDFATHER CLOCK.

Polly Flinder(s)　　*1 Cinder(s)*
Often used to describe over cooked food, e.g., 'This sausage is burnt to a Polly Flinder.'

2 Window(s)
A shiner's (window cleaner's) term.

Polly Parrot　　*Carrot*
A piece that could be a put off for a vegetarian.

Pony & Trap　　*Crap*
A very well established term both in reference to excrement and defecation whereby to go for a 'pony' has become commonplace. Also employed in connection with rubbish or bad merchandise. Anything that could be described as crappy can be 'pony'.

Poor Relation　　*Station*
Formed, presumably, when rich relations had cars but is hardly relevant these days when almost every family has a motor and even the rich find rail travel expensive.

Popcorn
Horn (Erection)
Quite common and generally abbreviated to a 'poppy'.

Pope of Rome
Home
An ancient term for where the heart is.

Popeye the Sailor
Tailor
Based on the cartoon character this is a more recent rival to that other old salt SINBAD THE SAILOR (qv).

Pop goes the Weasel
Diesel
A bit of a mouthful so always reduced to 'pop'. An example from the haulage trade.

Pork & Beans
Portuguese
Developed by soldiers of the 14–18 war.

Pork Chop(s)
Cops
A reference to the police that goes hand in cuff with the common slang for Mr Plod and Co, i.e., 'Pigs'.

Pork Pie(s)
Lie(s)
Enjoys nationwide popularity courtesy of TV exposure, often in the form of 'porkies'.

Porky Pig
Big
Used in terms of size and as a mild rebuke against someone who have done you no favours but thinks he has, e.g., 'Oh, so you've put my name down for a fiver's worth of raffle tickets have you? Well that was Porky pig of you.'

Port & Brandy
Randy
An appropriate piece since this concoction may be used by the saloon bar Lothario as a knickers loosener for his girlfriend.

Postage Stamp
Ramp
The ramp is another expression for the bar, therefore, 'Come on, get up the postage', means 'It's your round'.

Postman's Knock
Clock
Probably formed on the basis that you could set your 'postman's' by the postman's knock.

Pot & Pan　　*Man*
Always preceded by 'old' and meaning a husband or father. Known in backslang as the 'delo nam'.

Potatoes in the Mould　　*Cold*
Very well known and never said as anything other than 'taters'. Often preceded by bloody, bleeding, or, depending on the severity of the temperature, something stronger.

Pot of Glue　　*1 Jew*
Normally known as a 'potter'.

2 Queue
Not uncommon to get stuck in a 'pot of glue' in the post office on pension day.

Pot of Honey　　*Money*
One of several terms linking honey with the filthy lucre.

Pot(s) & Dish(es)　　*Wishes*
As granted by a genie from the East (End). A theatrical piece probably from a pantomime.

Pound Note　　*Coat*
An elderly piece that was based on the bank note that now lines the pockets of the great banker in the sky.

Pounds & Pence　　*Sense*
An updated version of SHILLINGS & PENCE in reference to a 'candidate for the van', e.g., 'If he had a bit more pounds and pence he'd just be daft.'

Powdered Chalk　　*Walk*
A less exercised version of the well known BALL OF CHALK (qv).

Pride & Joy　　*Boy*
Mainly a reference to a new born son and used for as long as he is the apple of his parents' eyes.

Prussian Guard　　*Card*
A playing card and a term for a bingo card that was formed when the game was still called housey-housey.

Pudding & Gravy   *Navy*
The 'pudding' is one of several terms for the senior service.

Pudding(s) & Pie(s)   *Eye(s)*
They may be tasty but they don't appear on the RS menu very often.

Puff & Drag   *Fag*
An alternative to COUGH & DRAG (qv) that is employed in the same way.

Punch & Judy   *Moody*
An example of slang for slang (*see* MOODY & SANKEY) and employed in disbelief at a story, e.g., 'Don't give me all that old Punch and Judy.'

Push in the Truck   *Fuck*
Refers only to coitus and was naturally developed in the transport industry.

Put & Take   *Cake*
An obsolete piece based on a defunct gambling game.

Quaker Oat *Coat*
Based on a brand of porridge which is synonymous with warmth, as is a coat.

Quarter Past Two *Jew*
Another of the multitude of terms regarding the non gentile. This one vies with:

Quarter To Two *Jew*
See previous entry.

Quasimodo *Soda (water)*
Reduced to 'quasi' or pronounced 'Quasimoda' for the traditional partner of (Bells?) whisky.

Queen of the South *Mouth*
Used as an alternative to the over worked NORTH & SOUTH (qv). Based on a Scottish football team which to the English is just a place on a pools coupon.

Queens Park Ranger(s) *Stranger(s)*
Although this is employed as a variant of GLASGOW RANGER (qv), it is used on a wider basis than that term. It is the non regular punter in a betting shop who strikes a large bet, the mysterious face in the pub, the person children shouldn't take sweets from and the little star of a happy event.

Rabbit & Pork   *Talk*
One of the superstars of RS. Always reduced to 'rabbit', it has now acquired a piece of slang of its own. Where once a person was said to have 'too much rabbit' he now has 'too much bunny'.

Rabbit Hutch   *Crutch (Crotch)*
A reference to the private parts, which gives a new meaning to a rabbit punch.

Radio Ones   *Runs (Diarrhoea)*
This just has to be an allusion to the verbal outpourings of your average DJ.

Radio Rental   *Mental*
A modern piece often heard on television in reference to a person with his or her 'hat on crooked'.

Raffle Ticket   *Ricket (Mistake)*
Usually employed by the person who has made the mistake, e.g., 'I've made a right raffle. I thought the favourite was in trap 6 and I backed the wrong dog.'

Rag & Bone   *Throne*
This is a reference to the lavatory seat and has nothing to do with where HM sits. At least, not when she is being regal. Strange to think of the Queen sitting on the toilet. Of course she does though. We've all heard of the royal flush and the royal wee is legendary.

Rain(ing) &   *Snore/Snoring*
Pour(ing)   Always reduced to the first element, e.g., 'You kept me awake all night with your raining.'

Raleigh Bike   *Dyke*
Probably based on the saying that purports to sum up a lesbian, i.e., 'I bet her bike's got a crossbar.'

Ralph Lynn   *Gin*
This predecessor of namesake VERA (qv) is named after an actor who was noted for his performances in farce. The term seems to have died along with the man, which was in 1964 (b. 1882).

Ramsgate Sand(s)   *Hand(s)*
The 'maulers' are fairly well known as 'Ramsgates'.

Randolph Scott   *Spot*
To have a face full of 'Randolphs' is the bane of youth. Based on the perennial goodie of countless western films. (1903–87).

Rangoon   *Prune*
Possibly based on the similar effect both are said to have on the bowel.

Ranjitiki   *Tricky*
A docker's term for an awkward situation based on the name of a cargo ship that used to berth at the Royal Albert Dock.

Raquel Welch   *Belch*
Just goes to show that nothing is sacred in RS. This glamorous film star, the sex goddess of her age, lends her name to an expulsion of gas from the stomach and all I can say is, Ms Welch, pardon!

Rasher & Bubble   *Double*
Applies mainly to a double on a dart board. The term is a dish of bacon with bubble and squeak.

Raspberry Ripple(s)   *Nipple(s)*
A bit of a mouthful, so these little bits are known as 'raspberries'.

Raspberry Tart

1 Fart
A piece that has joined the ranks of mainstream English but as an oral impression of the anal emission. 'Raspberries' are now blown rather than dropped.

2 Heart
The original employment for the term but now obsolete in this sense.

Rat & Mouse

1 House
An old piece that is as relevant today in many parts of London as it was on its formation.

2 Louse
This refers to a human louse, usually an informer.

Ratcatcher's Daughter

Water
An ancient example that has probably had its last utterance.

Rats & Mice

1 Dice
Very old term used by gamblers, e.g., 'The rats aint running for me tonight.'

2 Rice
Served up in curry houses where chicken and 'rats' is much ordered.

Rattlesnakes

Shakes
A case of the Delirium Tremens (DTs) whereby the 'rattles' follow the morning after being rattled (drunk).

Rat Trap

Jap
Reduced to a 'rat' this is a World War Two term that mustn't be used today. Try telling that to an ex-POW.

Rawalpindi

Windy
Based on the name of a passenger liner that regularly berthed at London's Royal Docks. With the advent of World War Two she was commandeered by the Royal Navy and converted into an armed merchant cruiser. On 23 November 1939 she gallantly but suicidally engaged two of Germany's most powerful battle cruisers, *Gneisenau* and *Scharnhorst*. With the sinking of *Rawalpindi* 265 members of her crew were lost. The term therefore is a reference to weather conditions, definitely

not cowardice.

Razor Blade — *Spade*
An offensive reference to a black person, often slashed to 'razor'.

Razzmatazz — *Jazz*
Refers to this type of music and the noisy excitement generated by it. Especially when played traditionally.

Read & Write — *Fight*
Never used in truncated form. Two people having a 'read' doesn't conjure up visions of violence so they therefore have a right old 'read and write'.

Red Devil — *Level*
A spirit level as used by tradesmen.

Red Hots — *Trots (Diarrhoea)*
During a bout of the 'scatters' the term is aptly descriptive of the muzzle of one's 'scatter gun'. Namely the anus.

Red Rum — *Dumb*
Most commonly used in regard to people who can speak but don't, rather than those who can't, e.g., 'Why didn't you say something, you're not Red Rum are you?'

Reeling & Rockings — *Stockings*
Developed during the rock'n'roll era and inspired by the twirling of girls in loose skirts thus revealing their nylon clad legs.

Reels of Cotton — *Rotten*
Refers to the putrefication of food or a state of affairs that has gone wrong, e.g., 'The job was OK once but since they stopped the overtime it's all gone reels of cotton.'

Reggie & Ronnie — *Johnny (Condom)*
A case of the brothers Kray still offering protection.

Reverend Ronald Knox — *Pox (VD)*
A sacrilegious offering alluding to all types of the disease that this catholic priest could never have caught. Given that he did his job properly. Truncated to the 'right reverend' or the 'reverend Ronald' it is based on an

actual holy man who also wrote detective stories (1888–
1957).

Rhubarb(s)   *Sub(s)*
This is always pronounced 'rhubub' and refers to an advance of wages or a loan. With the final 's' it applies to subscriptions, as paid by club members, often local football or darts clubs. 'Subs' is also a shortening of suburbs for which 'rhubarbs' is used by cab drivers, the suburbs being part of the knowledge.

Ribbon & Curl   *Girl*
An example for a little girl that needs no explanation.

Richard Burton(s)   *Curtain(s)*
Named after the great thespian (1925–84) this relates both to the theatrical and domestic curtain.

Richard the Third   *1 Bird*
Originally applied to the feathered variety but became widely used in connection with young ladies where it is always 'Richards'. It also applies to the 'bird' as given to second rate performers.

2 Turd
Of secondary usage but quite common.

3 Word
Hardly ever employed but to give one's oath is to give one's 'Richard'.

Richard Todd   *Cod*
A localized piece and used only in relation to a portion of fried cod. Named after the British actor.

Riddle-me-Ree   *Pee/Wee*
Only ever used in full as the first element sounds too much like piddle.

Riff Raff   *Taff*
A reference to a Welsh person which some may consider apt.

Rifle Range   *Change*
A reference to what women check, men lose, children spend and taxi drivers keep.

Rinky Dink   *Pink*
Used in connection with a snooker ball and as a term of well being, i.e., 'in the pink'.

Rip & Tear   *Swear*
Another term that has ventured beyond the bounds of RS. As a result of a loss of temper, a person may sound off with a barrage of bad language. That person is said to be 'letting rip'.

Rip Van Winkle   *Tinkle/Sprinkle (Urinate)*
Tinkle is a youngster's euphemism, while sprinkle is more adult.

Rise & Shine   *Wine*
Not a particularly apt example as a Bacchanalian hangover is as bad as any you can get.

Rising Damp   *Cramp*
Common among sports people especially Sunday morning footballers.

Riverina   *Deaner (5p)*
A term of old currency that survives today. A deaner was an ultra common name for a shilling and is still relevant to its modern day equivalent.

River Lea   *Tea*
A very old piece based on the East End's other river. Often applied to a particularly bad cup of tea.

River Nile   *Smile*
A glum person may be told, 'Come on, put your boat in the River Nile.' *See* BOAT RACE.

River Ouse   *Booze*
A common expression for being out drinking is to be on the river Ouse.

River Tyne   *Wine*
Refers to a bottle from the cheaper end of the wine list. It wouldn't do to call a vintage Burgundy a bottle of 'river Tyne'.

Roach & Dace   *Face*

Less common variant of KIPPER & PLAICE (qv).

Roast Beef　　*Teeth*
Sometimes applied in a violent mode, e.g., 'I'll knock your roast beef so far down your throat you'll be able to eat your dinner again.'

Roast Pork　　*1 Fork*
Applies to the kitchen utensil and could conceivable be used to confuse a lost motorist, e.g., 'Keep going till you come to a roast pork and chuck an Isle o' Wight.'

2 Talk
A teller of tall stories may be told, 'You don't half roast a load of rubbish,' or asked, 'What the hell are you roasting about?'

Roast Potato　　*Waiter*
One of several terms rhyming waiter and potato. This one is usually decreased to a 'roastie'.

Robert E Lee(s)　　*1 Knee(s)*
Generally the American Civil War soldier is disjointed to 'Robert' or 'Robert E' and often in connection with a painful one and based on the commander of the Confederate armies in the US Civil War. (1807–70)

2 Quay
An elderly piece coined by dock workers.

Robin Hood(s)　　*1 Good(s)*
An appropriate example since it is based on the legendary goodie and can be seen in a number of guises. It is what children are forever being told to be. It may be used sarcastically, possibly to someone who has volunteered your services without your knowledge, e.g., 'Oh that was Robin Hood of you.' In terms of uselessness, things may be 'no Robin Hood' and when pluralized refers to merchandise.

2 Wood(s)
Fittingly relates to a collection of trees or a chopped up one. Was also a schoolboy expression for Woodbine cigarettes as sold singly, i.e., 'a tup'ney Robin Hood'.

Robinson Crusoe　　*Do so*

Used defiantly in response to a threat, e.g., 'If you don't move your car from in front of my gate I'll call the police.' 'Well Robinson Crusoe.'

Rock(s) & Boulder(s)   *Shoulder(s)*
Significant of the strong variety on which a weaker soul may lean.

Rock'n'Roll   *1 Dole*
Most up to date of many terms for being unemployed is to be on the 'rock'n'roll'.

2 Hole
Clothes, boots, or excuses may be full of 'rock'n'rolls'.

Rocking Horse   *Sauce*
Applies to the condiment and also to cheek. Liberty takers may be told, 'You've got some bloody rocking horse you have.'

Rock of Ages   *Wages*
Based on an old hymn and commonly known as 'rocks'.

Rogue & Villain   *Shilling*
An old monetary piece that is now well spent.

Roll me in the Gutter   *Butter*
An ancient example that has always been known as 'roll me'.

Rolls Royce   *Voice*
Applies, naturally enough, to a superior singing voice.

Roman Candle(s)   *Sandal(s)*
Fittingly known as 'Romans'.

Ronnie Biggs   *Digs (Lodgings)*
Named after the train robber who, not satisfied with his own living conditions, left and sought fresh digs. In Brazil.

Rookery Nook   *Book*
Known as a 'rookery' this is based on the name of an old Aldwych farce.

Rory O'More   *1 Door*
An ancient entry that is still in frequent use.

2 Floor
Main employment for this is in the sense of being destitute, e.g., 'on the Rory', which is almost another case of slang for slang. *See* ON THE FLOOR.

Rosebud(s)   *Spud(s)*
Common and often mashed to 'roses'.

Roses Red   *Bed*
An uncommon alternative to UNCLE NED (qv).

Rosie Lee   *Tea*
An evergreen term for the drink that English people wash down the troubles of the world with.

Rotten Row   *Blow*
Refers to being struck, e.g., 'a Rotten Row to the back of the head'.

Round the Houses   *Trousers*
A very familiar piece that is usually dropped to 'round de's'. The term is sometimes given as 'round me houses' in which case 'round me's' is the diminutive.

Royal Docks   *Pox (VD)*
Apart from the disease this also applies to being irritated by a situation. Long stationary motorists on the M25 may utter 'I've got the Royal Docks of this.'

Royal Mail   *Bail*
Almost exclusively the property of the criminal fraternity.

Royal Navy   *Gravy*
An alternative to the more popular ARMY & NAVY (qv) and maybe based on the adage 'the navy gets the gravy but the army gets the beans'.

Roy Hudd   *Blood*
Only heard this once but the story is worth telling.

A less than funny comedian was struggling to get laughs in an East End pub on a Sunday lunchtime. He was heckled, abused and harassed and somebody or other would shout the punchline to every joke he tried to tell. In the end it all became too much for him and, unable to take any more, he held up his handkerchief as a white flag of surrender which incurred even more derision. With a tear in his eye he pleaded with his audience. 'Look,' he said, 'I'm doing my best. What do you want Roy Hudd?' 'Yes,' replied a wag and launched a light ale bottle in the direction of the funny man's head. He never appeared there again.

Roy Rogers　　*Bodgers*
Applicable to 'cowboy' tradesmen and suitably based on the name of the western film star who was billed as the King of the Cowboys.

Rub-a-Dub-Dub　　*1 Club*
A working man's or a night club is indicated here. Also the suit in a pack of cards.

2 Pub
Taken from the nursery rhyme about the three men in a tub, this enjoys extensive usage generally in the abbreviated forms of 'rubber' or 'rubber dub'. sometimes said as 'Rub-a-Di-Dub' which breaks down to 'rubbidy'.

3 Sub
A less used variant of RHUBARB (qv) in respect of an advance on wages.

Rubber Duck　　*Fuck*
Only employed in the sense of not caring. Not to give a 'monkeys' is 'I couldn't give a rubber duck.' Possibly from the hit record of 1976, *Convoy* by C W McCall, in which the term was the call sign used by a truck driver on his CB radio.

Ruby Rose　　*Nose*
Always truncated to the first element which may often be quite suitable.

Ruby Murray　　*Curry*
Based on the name of an Irish songstress a 'Ruby' has become a common expression for a 'ringburner'.

Ruck & Row　　*Cow*

Refers to a disagreeable woman and not the animal. Often reduced to the first element and prefaced with 'old', as in 'the old ruck next door'.

Ruin & Spoil   *Oil*
Fittingly abridged to 'ruin' and probably coined in the wake of all the environmental damage caused by the spillage of the stuff.

Runner & Rider   *Cider*
Sounds as though this may have been formed on a west country race track.

Rupert Bear(s)   *Share(s)*
A modern example, formed since the sell off of some of the nationalized industries to the general public. Reduced to 'Ruperts' which seems quite suitable, this being a name that can easily be associated with the stock exchange.

Russell Harty   *Party*
This was in vogue for a short while but seems to have died along with this TV presenter, (1934–88).

Russian Duck   *Fuck*
A reference to the sex act.

Sad & Sorry   *Lorry*
A rueful sounding piece for the overgrown mini.

Safe & Sound   *Ground*
Possibly made up by a nervous air traveller who was only too happy to get his feet back on the 'safe'.

Saint & Sinner   *Dinner*
Connotations of Sunday dinner time when the saint cooks while the sinner goes to the pub, has a skinful, comes home, noisily wolfs his meal then crashes out in the armchair.

St Louis Blues   *Shoes*
Based on the title of a jazz song and abbreviated to 'St Louis', this may have its roots in the theatre.

St Martins-le-Grand(s)   *Hand(s)*
The extended version of MARTIN-LE-GRAND (qv) is always decreased to 'St Martins'.

Salford Docks   *Rocks*
A piece of nautical slang for those navigational hazards around the coastline.

Salmon & Trout   *1 Gout*
In this guise the term is probably more common than the disease.

2 Snout

This applies to snout in all its forms including the nose, an informer and a cigarette.

3 Stout
Refers to this type of beer rather than the waistline that may occur through drinking it.

Tout
Originally a race course term regarding somebody selling information. Now it also applies to those who sell over priced tickets.

Salt Junk

Drunk
Quite well known in reduced form of 'salted' which is very old and called after the salted beef fed to the soldiers of a previous era.

Salvation

Station
Ancient reference to where the Lord's name is uttered by more people every day than anywhere else.

Salvation Army

Barmy
Nearly always truncated to 'sally army' in relation to a person who may also be known as 'silly boy got none'.

Sammy Halls

Balls (Testicles)
This is taken from a similar song to the one described in NOBBY HALLS (qv).

Sandy McNab

Cab
A post war term for a taxi.

Sandy McNabs

Crabs (Crab Lice)
A fairly common alternative to the unfortunate BEATTIE & BABS (qv).

Sandy Powell

Towel
One of several members of the Powell clan to forge this link, this one being the late northern comedian. Not long before his death in 1982, the same age as the century, he performed his famous ventriloquist sketch on television which is one of the all-time classic pieces of comedy.

San Toy(s)

Boy(s)
Based on the name of an early 20th century play, this is pertinent to gang members or 'the boys'. Which may or

S

may not be sinister.

Satin & Silk *Milk*
An ad-man's dream of a term, describing the richness and smoothness of the product.

Sausage & Mash *1 Cash*
To have 'eaten my last bit of sausage' or the more widely used 'I haven't got a sausage' are two phrases that point to empty pockets.

2 Crash/Smash
This is cab driver's jargon for a road traffic accident.

Sausage Roll *1 Pole*
Applies in all senses of the word. To drive someone up the 'sausage' is to drive him mad. To perform the sex act (to pole) is to 'sausage' and a polish person is a 'sausage roll'.

2 Poll (Head)
A recent extension to (1) includes the hated poll tax and those that led the Labour party up the garden path in the run up to the 1992 general election.

Saucepan Lid *1 Kid*
Kids are always known as 'saucepans' be they your own little darlings or the pests playing knock down Ginger, who may be known as 'bleeding saucepans'. Also employed in the guise of deception. The mock innocent pleadings of a conman may include 'Would I try to saucepan you?'

2 Quid
The first element is often quoted for £1.

3 Yid
A not uncommon piece although one of many for a Jew.

Saveloy *Boy*
Used to describe a small boy but sometimes as a rival to SAN TOY (qv).

Savoury Rissole *Piss Hole*
Refers, naturally enough, to a lavatory but not exclusively. Any place that can be described as a dump, be it a pub, club, cinema or even a town, can be referred to

as a 'savoury rissole'.

Say Goodbye　　*Die*
This is as fitting as any term here included since it's what we'll all do one day.

Scabby Eye　　*Pie*
A pie filled with fat and gristle.

Scapa Flow　　*Go*
Scarper is a very common piece of slang meaning a hasty exit, that has long held a place in the annals of RS. It is however just as, if not more, likely to be another item of parlyaree, the slang based on the Italian language, in which scapare means to runaway or escape. Scapa Flow is a stretch of sea in the Orkney islands where 71 surrendered German warships were scuttled in June 1919.

Scotch Egg(s)　　*Leg(s)*
An updated version of the ancient SCOTCH PEGS (qv), the difference being that this is used in full.

Scotch Mist　　*Pissed (Drunk)*
An ultra familiar piece that is never used half cut. One is always 'scotch mist'.

Scotch Peg(s)　　*Leg(s)*
The original version of SCOTCH EGGS (qv) that is always truncated to 'scotch' or 'scotches'.

Scraggy Lou　　*Flu*
How a woman who normally takes pride in her appearance will describe herself when she is riddled with flu germs: 'I've got the scraggy Lou and I look like her.' Who the lady was is not recorded.

Scrambled Egg(s)　　*Leg(s)*
Mainly used in terms of drunkenness. To have 'scrambled eggs' is to be blotto.

Scrap Metal　　*Kettle*
An example once found in building site canteens and usually shortened to the first element.

Screwdriver　　*Skiver*

A reference to the person who knows what needs to be done and how to get out of doing it. Since the contents of a toolbag are a complete mystery to him the term doesn't appear to be pertinent.

Sebastian Coe(s) *Toe(s)*
A very recent piece that is used in the context of making a quick getaway. To 'have it on your Sebastians (or Sebs)' is to do a runner 'a bit lively'. A totally suitable piece given the man's talent for running. In 1992 he successfully ran for parliament being elected MP for Falmouth and Camborne.

Seldom Seen *Queen*
A reference to the present monarch which seems reasonably apt.

Selina Scott(s) *Spot(s)*
An updated version of RANDOLPH SCOTT (qv) whereby sproot covered juveniles are actually 'Selina' covered juveniles. Names after the British TV personality.

Semolina *Cleaner*
Applies to a person who re-arranges dust on a professional basis.

Seven & Six *Fix*
To be in difficulty is to be in a 'right old seven and six'. It also applies to putting something right, e.g., 'Leave it to your old man, he'll seven and six it.'

Seven Dials *Piles*
An allusion to that painful condition sometimes colourfully known as 'grapes'.

Sexton Blake *1 Cake*
A long established piece based on the name of a fictional detective.

2 Fake
Refers to a forgery or copy, especially a painting. Tom Keating, the master copier of old masters, often referred to his works as 'Sexton Blakes'.

Shake & Shiver *River*

Generally dammed at the first element as in 'messing about on the shake'.

Sharp & Blunt　　*Cunt*
Employed only in a vulgar anatomical sense.

Shell Mex　　*Sex*
Based on the name of the oil company, to have 'blagged a bit of shell mex' is to have achieved a successful pull.

Shepherd's Bush　　*Push*
Chopped to the 'Shepherd's' in reference to *the* push, i.e., the sack.

Shepherd's Pie　　*Sky*
Reduced to the first element, this would appear to be connected with the red sky at night.

Sherbet Dip　　*Tip (Gratuity)*
An appropriate piece since in cockney parlance a tip is often referred to as a drink. And a drink is known as a 'sherbet'.

Sherman Tank　　*1 Wank (Masturbate)*
A fairly common example that has recently been transferred from its original meaning, namely:
2 Yank
A 'Sherman' is our cousin across the pond.

Shillings & Pence　　*Sense*
A very old reference to a dopey dratsab is 'He aint got the shillings he was born with.'

Shiny & Bright　　*All Right*
A state of satisfaction is quoted as 'all shiny'.

Ship in Full Sail　　*Pint of Ale*
This term is as old as it suggests. Always truncated to the first element whereby a pint has long been known as a 'ship'. Incidentally, a pint of ale in backslang becomes a 'teenip of ella'.

Shirt & Collar　　*Dollar*
An elderly allusion to what is now 25p, which may be responsible for the racegoer having his shirt on a good

thing. Sometimes known as a 'Shirt Collar'.

Shoes & Socks
Pox (VD)
The 'shoes' is another name for the sexual blight.

Shout & Holler
Collar
A more recent rival to HOLLER BOYS HOLLAR (qv) but still pretty old.

Shove & Broom
Room
A 'shovel' is a reference to a room, not to space.

Shovel & Pick
1 Mick
Refers to an Irishman, mainly a building site worker which makes the piece totally suitable.

2 Nick
Prison is known as 'the shovel'.

Shovel & Spade
Blade
Cut to a 'shovel' and used in the same way as FIRST AID (qv).

Shower Bath
Half
A term coined on the race track originally in reference to ten shillings (half a pound). Always known as a 'showers' it has made the transition to 50p.

Silas Hockings
Stockings
A term formed in the theatre on the name of an author.

Silent Night
Light (Ale)
A form of CHRISTMAS CHEER (qv) inspired by a carol.

Silver Spoon
Moon
Generally referred to as 'the silver'.

Silvery Moon
Coon
Reduced to the first element this is another abusive term for a black person.

Simple Simon
Diamond
Applies to the precious stone and the not so valuable playing card. Unless you're holding five of them. Occasionally used when ordering a pint of (Double)

Diamond.

Sinbad the Sailor *Tailor*
Old but largely unheard piece due to the popularity of casual dress and the wide availability of off the peg suits.

Sir Anthony Blunt *Cunt*
There are many terms for the C word but this one takes it to its most objectionable. It applies to a horrible scaly backed reptile of a person, e.g., 'He's an out and out, no good Sir Anthony and I hate him.' May also give a new slant to the Tony awards. Based on the name of a British traitor (1907–83). The word in backslang appears as 'teenuc' but is pronounced 'tinnuc'.

Sir Walter Scott *Pot*
Another piece from the world of the drinking classes, this applies to a pint pot. Based on the novelist and poet who died in 1832.

Sit Beside Her *Spider*
Common when houses had outdoor lavatories wherein lurked many an arachnid to keep a person company.

Six & Eight *1 State (of Agitation)*
A complete counterpart of TWO & EIGHT (qv) which is a much more familiar expression.

2 Straight
A reference to a person who can be trusted.

Six Months Hard *Card*
An out of date bingo card.

Six To Four *Whore*
Coined possibly, on the odds on catching something from one.

Skin & Blister *Sister*
Relatively speaking this is an extensively used piece.

Skinny as a Broom *Groom*
Jokingly dislengthened to a 'skinny' as he stands at the alter with his FAT & WIDE (qv). Both terms come from the

comic verse made to fit the Wedding March.

Skip & Jump   *Pump*
A descriptively appropriate allusion to the heart.

Sky Diver   *Fiver (£5)*
A modern alternative to LADY GODIVA (qv).

Skylark   *Park*
A suitable example since the park is where people go to lark about. Sometimes used in regard to parking a car, e.g., 'Sorry I'm late but I couldn't find anywhere to skylark.'

Sky Rocket   *Pocket*
A widely employed piece, often in the first element.

Skyscraper   *Paper*
Applies to all types of paper, including writing, toilet and what your chips come wrapped in.

Slap & Tickle   *Pickle*
Relates to the edible kind rather that a predicament.

Slice of Ham   *Gam (Fellatio)*
A rare alternative to the widely used PLATE OF HAM (qv).

Slice of Toast   *Ghost*
Sometimes used as an embellishment to the old cliché: 'What's the matter? You look like you've seen a slice of toast.'

Slug(s) & Snail(s)   *Nail(s)*
Applies to the finger or toe nail and is normally cut to 'slugs' often to a habitual nail biter in the hope of putting him or her off.

Smack in the Eye   *Pie*
Care should be taken when ordering one of these in a pub. If the barman is big and thick, don't!

Smash & Grab   *Cab*
Applies to either a minicab or a black one. Probably most effective in reference to the latter as one often needs to pull off a robbery to be able to pay the fare.

Smile & Smirk   *Work*
Usually cut to the first element whereby you may be 'smiling' if you are employed or out of 'smile' if you're not.

Smoked Haddock   *Paddock*
An example from the racing game.

Snakes Hiss   *Piss*
Used only in connection with urination.

Snog & Fuck   *Dog & Duck*
This is an inside joke used by office workers in the City of London for a near-by pub which allegedly had a reputation for being a meeting place for bosses and secretaries. I suppose I should stress the words 'meeting place' as much bunking in the snug is not suggested.

Snoop & Pry   *Cry*
The cause of many a midnight argument is a 'snooping' baby.

Snoozing & Snoring   *Boring*
An obvious but appropriate offering that is mostly reduced to 'snoozing' and sometimes 'snooze & snoring'.

Snow & Ice   *Price*
Said with some trepidation at the expense of an article: 'But look at the snow and ice of it.' Also refers, perhaps more commonly, to starting prices.

Snow Whites   *Tights*
Applies to the legwear favoured by women but not men.

Soap & Flannel   *Panel*
Being out of work through ill health is still known as being on the 'soap and flannel'. For explanation *see* ENGLISH CHANNEL.

Soap & Lather   *Father*
For third party use only when talking about your old man. Also makes the pope the 'holy soap'.

Soap & Water	*Daughter* Should be used in full to differentiate from the previous entry.
Soldier Ants	*Pants* A reference to underwear, 'soldiers' for short(s).
Soldier Bold	*Cold* Very old term for the illness, known as 'catching a soldier'.
Song and Dance	*Chance* Always used in full. A flat refusal is said as, 'You've got no song and dance.' A request becomes, 'Any song and dance of a sub till the weekend?'
Song of the Thrush	*Brush* An ancient piece for any type of brush. Also, to give somebody the 'song of the thrush' is to give him or her the brush off.
Sorrowful Tale	*Jail* An old but still appropriate term when applied to the tales of misfortune as told by convicts. These stories may range from a deprived upbringing to a flat tyre on the getaway car.
Sorry & Sad	*Bad* Very well known piece. Anything in a bad way is said to be in a 'sorry state'.
Soup & Gravy	*Navy* Known by sailors as being in the 'soup'.
Southend-on-Sea	*Pee/Wee* A term for 'having one up the wheel' that was probably coined on a beano by a bunch of drunken day trippers who kept stopping the coach to do just that.
Southend Pier(s)	*Ear(s)* Presumably the sticking out kind.
South of France	*Dance* Applies to both the physical act of dancing and to a social event, an invitation to which sounds irresistible.

South Pole *Hole (Anus)*
The more fitting variant of NORTH POLE (qv).

Spanish Guitar *Cigar*
Commonly stubbed to a 'Spanish'.

Spanish Main *Drain*
Money lost or wasted may be referred to as 'money down the Spanish'.

Spanish Onion *Bunion*
An apposite piece since this painful swelling may resemble an onion.

Spanish Waiter *Potato*
Roast, boil, sauté or mash. Some of the many things to do with a 'Spanish waiter'. But on a package holiday to the Costas it's mainly chips.

Spit & Drag *Fag*
A variation on the theme of COUGH & DRAG (qv).

Sporting Life *Wife*
Either based on the racing paper or the person who coined it had an exhaustive training programme.

Spotted Dick *Sick*
Not necessarily as nasty as it sounds. It can be used as an alternative to TOM & DICK (qv) or can apply to a portion of re-gurge seen lying on the pavement.

Sprasi Anna *Tanner*
Another term that has been consigned to that great money box in the sky. A 'sprasi' (pronounced sprar-sey) was sixpence in our former coinage that survived decimalization for a while as 2½p.

Squad Halt *Salt*
A military piece that stems from the 14–18 war. Therefore a seasoned campaigner in the service of RS.

Square Rigger *Nigger*
An offensive term that may have originated in the docks.

Stage Fright　　*Light (Ale)*
A nerve settler for the entertainer, a piece that hails from the theatre.

Stammer & Stutter　*Butter*
Probably the commonest term for the unhealthiest bread spread. *See also* NEEDLE & THREAD.

Stand at Ease　　*Cheese*
Another example that grew out of the trenches during the great war.

Stand from Under　*Thunder*
The term is a warning used by people working at a height when something is to be dropped to the ground. It is therefore an aptish piece.

Stand to Attention　*Pension*
Originally referred to an ex-soldier's pension but has found its way into civvy street.

Steak & Kidney　*Sidney*
Shortened to 'steak' to join the élite band of Christian names to have a term of RS. Australians use it as a reference to Sydney.

Steak & Kidney Pie　*Eye*
Hasn't knocked MINCE PIE (qv) off the menu.

Steamroller　　*Bowler (Hat)*
A dying piece simply because the headwear of the typical city gent is all but a thing of the past.

Steam Tug　　*1 Bug*
With modern hygiene the term 'steamers' is now thankfully obsolete except in older people's ramblings about the 'good old days'.

2 Mug
A 'right steamer' is a person easily taken in.

Stewart Grainger　*Danger*
Overheard in a city pub recently when a particularly slow barmaid was a cause of impatience among the clientele, one of whom remarked, 'Any Stewart Grainger of getting

177

pissed in here today?'

Stewed Prune   *Tune*
The job of the rapidly disappearing pub pianist is to play the 'stewed prunes' while the assembled inebriates attempt to 'mangle' them. *See* MANGLE & WRING.

Stick(s) & Stone(s)   *Bone(s)*
It's my fervent wish that you all make old 'sticks'. Nobody can ask for more than a long life and a short death.

Stick of Rock   *Cock*
This has absolutely nothing to do with poultry except maybe in reference to the last turkey in the shop. Often mentioned in talk of oral sex.

Stick Bun   *Son*
Applies to a small boy.

Stirling Moss   *Toss*
Can be used to signify something of little value. Of an untrustworthy person it may be said, 'He's not worth a Stirling Moss.' Also used in a sense of not caring, e.g., 'He don't give a Stirling about anyone but himself.'

Stocks & Shares   *Stairs*
A lesser known alternative to the much quoted APPLES & PEARS (qv).

Stoke on Trent   *Bent*
A fairly recent term for a homosexual.

Stop & Go(s)   *Toe(s)*
Often reduced to 'stop(s)' but normally used in full when trouble's afoot, that is when someone treads on your 'stop and go'.

Stop & Start   *Heart*
An anatomically relevant piece that needs no examination.

Stop Thief   *Beef*
An ancient piece that may, when it was coined, have been fitting. Food, especially meat, was an oft stolen commodity in Victorian London.

Strangely Weird   *Beard*
Generally shorn to the first element.

Strawberry Ripple   *Cripple*
A modern, unsympathetic example.

Strawberry Tart   *Heart*
Broken to a 'strawberry' possibly because of a resemblance.

Strike Me Dead   *Bread*
Mostly cut to a slice of 'strike me'.

String Beans   *Jeans*
Often shortened to 'strings'.

Struggle & Strain   *Train*
This was originally confined to the railway tracks but has also come to refer to physical exertion, which seems quite suitable.

Struggle & Strainers *Trainers*
'Struggles' are the footwear required to perform the exercises of the previous entry. They are also the overpriced necessity for fashion conscious teenagers who have to be seen wearing the right names on their feet.

Struggle & Strife   *1 Life*
If ever there was an appropriate term this is it. Unless you are one of the silver spoon brigade.

2 Wife
May be as apt as (1) given the right circumstances i.e. the wrong woman.

Stutter & Stammer   *Hammer*
Normally banged down to the first element.

Sugar & Honey   *Money*
Very old and widely used in the truncated form of 'sugar'.

Sugar & Spice   *1 Ice*
Mainly employed to describe the contents of an ice bucket.

2 Nice
Always decreased to 'sugar', this does not take on the sarcastic aspect of APPLES & RICE (qv).

Sugar Candy

1 Brandy
An archaic piece but one that is still in order.

2 Handy
The major employment for this is in the reverse sense. An umbrella with a hole in may be described as, 'That's bloody sugar candy that is.'

Sugar Stick

Prick (Penis)
A reference to the sex pistol that may loom large in talk of fellatio.

Sunday Best

Vest
Formed when this garment was restricted to underwear and only slobs ventured into the street in their 'Sunday bests'.

Sunday Morn

Horn (Erection)
Seems to be based on the only morning of the week when a working couple can take advantage of it.

Sunny South

Mouth
A largely unsung piece due to the fame of NORTH & SOUTH (qv).

Surrey Docks

Pox (VD)
Has an identical usage as ROYAL DOCKS (qv).

Swallow & Sigh

Collar & Tie
A rare example of a double word rhyme.

Swanee River

Liver
Applies both to the living human organ or that of a dead animal reclining on a slab in the butcher's shop.

Swan Lake

Cake
A cup of tea and a slice of 'swan'?

Swear & Cuss

Bus
Since millions of people do this every day whilst waiting for public transport, this is a particularly pertinent

piece.

Sweaty Sock   *Jock (Scot)*
Very common especially among young football supporters.

Sweeney Todd   *Flying Squad*
Named after the demon barber of Fleet Street whose contribution to *haute cuisine* was hair raising. He would
butcher his clients and sell their bodies to a pie maker.
Hence the expression 'Walls have ears'. On entering his
establishment his customers could have been said to have
had one foot in the gravy and ended up with their fingers
in many pies.

Swiftly Flowing   *Going*
An Australian piece that is included for its suitability in
the sense of rapid departure.

Syrup of Fig   *Wig*
'Syrups' normally stick out like a boil on the nose and
draw attention in the same way. The most obvious, so
therefore the worst, hairpieces are known as 'golden
syrups'.

Tapioca

Joker

Applies to the joker in a pack of cards.

Tar & Feather

Leather

Normally known as a 'tar' and refers to a leather jacket.

Tartan Banner

Tanner

A term from our previous currency, now consigned to history, that may turn up in a television costume drama.

Ta Ta Kiss

Piss

Used only in the mode of MICKY BLISS (qv) and is said as 'taking the ta ta'.

Tate & Lyle

Style

Mainly applies to a person with a lot of front or guiver, who, after getting away with an almighty liberty, may be told, often admiringly, 'You've got some Tate & Lyle you have.' Based on the sugar company with long held east London connections.

Taxi Cab(s)

Crab(s)

Applies to the sea food traditionally sold outside pubs on Sundays. It is also more unpleasantly employed as a reference to crab lice. A warning against going with a 'dodgy bird' is, 'Keep clear of her or you'll end up with the taxis.'

Taxi Rank

Wank (Masturbate)

A 'taxi' is one of many terms for 'one off the wrist'.

Tea & Cocoa *Say So*
A variant is COFFEE & COCOA (qv) that may be used in full, e.g., 'If you wanted to borrow some money why didn't you tea and cocoa?'

Tea & Toast *Post*
Applies to mail, e.g., 'Anything in the tea and toast this morning?'

Tea For Two *Jew*
Generally cut to a 'teafer'.

Tea For Two & A Bloater *Motor*
A term that was formed as a condescending term for the 'new fangled horseless carriage' and is now obviously obsolete. Its inclusion is simply down to the fact that I like it.

Tea Grout *Scout*
An example for a boy scout that is secondary to BRUSSELS SPROUT (qv).

Tea Leaf *Thief*
The commonest term for the sticky fingered villain and one that is never shortened.

Tea Pot Lid *1 Kid 2 Quid 3 Yid*
In all cases identical to SAUCEPAN LID (qv).

Tea Strainers *Trainers*
Another reference to those items of footwear described at STRUGGLE & STRAINERS (qv).

Teddy Bear *Pear*
An offering from the fruit market.

Ted Heath *1 Teeth 2 Thief*
For both definitions *see* EDWARD HEATH.

Tennis Racket *Jacket*
Shortened to the first element and sounds like it must allude to a sports jacket.

Ten to Two *Jew*
For whom we have terms in abundance already.

Tent Peg   *Egg*
An eggsrutiatingly uneggciting eggsample.

Terrible Turk   *Work*
Employed by those for whom work is a four letter word.

Tex Ritter   *Bitter (Ale)*
Formed on the name of an old time western film star and ordered as a 'pint of Tex'. Born in 1907, Mr Ritter's last round up came in 1974.

That & This   *Piss*
Used only in connection with water production.

Thelonius Monk   *Spunk (Semen)*
A localized piece that comes down to the Christian name of this jazz pianist.

There You Are   *1 Bar*
An old example rarely used in this form.

Char (Tea)
More likely to be heard in this guise, e.g., 'There you are, a nice cup of there you are.'

These & Those   *1 Clothes*
A piece that is never worn short, always shop for some 'these and those'.

2 Toes
A pluralistic term for the tootsies.

Theydon Bois   *Noise*
Named after a village on the edge of Epping Forest which once constituted a day out for the poor children of London. They would be taken there on school or Sunday school outings and given a taste of life away from the slums. Let loose in the country they would have made quite a bit of 'Theydon Bois'.

Thick & Thin   *1 Chin*
On which a big man is expected to take it.

2 Gin
The spirit of London revisited.

Thimble & Thumb *Rum*
Shortened to a 'tot of thimble'.

This & That *1 Bat*
an ancient reference to a cricket bat.

2 Hat
A piece that is always used in its full extension but is inferior to TIT FOR TAT (qv).

Thomas Tilling *Shilling*
One of many terms for this extinct sum of money. However, to many people 5p will always be a shilling so maybe 'Thomas' still has a currency somewhere. But I doubt it. In the 19th century Mr Tilling had a large horse-drawn transport business.

Three Blind Mice *Rice*
An order of 'curried beef and three blind mice' may be a cause of great confusion to a Chinese or Indian waiter.

Threepenny Bit(s) *Tit(s)*
A term that still survives even though this particular coin died of decimalitis.

Tickle Your Fancy *Nancy (Homosexual)*
A post World War Two piece that may be from a corrupted version of a line in the song 'Billy Boy':
Did (a) nancy tickle your fancy
Oh my darling Billy boy.

Tic Tac *Fact*
When the world and its brother adopted BRASS TACK (qv) the cockney turned to this and TIN TACK (qv). In the racing world tic tac is a system of hand signals designed to show changes of odds from one ring to another. Outside the race track the term took a turn to mean any kind of signal, e.g., 'I'll make a move when you give me the tic tac.'

Tiddler's Bait *Late*
Often said as 'tiddley bait' sometimes in the form of an excuse, e.g., 'Sorry I'm Tiddley I met Cyril on the way home and he forced me to go for a drink.' This however is not a good excuse and will not prevent the sharp edge of a wife's tongue from tearing her hapless spouse to

shreds.

Tiddly Wink

1 Chink
A common reference to a Chinese person.

2 Drink
Normally reduced to the first element and is widely used in connection with alcohol whereby one may go for a little 'tiddly'. It is also extensively employed to describe the effects of drink and is a byword for being slightly inebriated.

Tidy & Neat

Eat
The only 'tidying up' kids will do is to the fridge. Only ever used in the first element, e.g., 'Tidy your dinner up first, then you can go out.'

Tilbury Docks

1 Pox (VD)
Commonly known as the 'Tilburys' and applies to all forms of what in backslang is the 'exop'.

2 Socks
A piece that originated in the navy but is rarely used in this guise because of the wide usage of (1).

Tin Bath

Scarf
Sometimes shrunk to 'tin' as an accompaniment to 'Titfer', e.g., 'It's freezing out so put your titfer and tin on.' *See* TIT FOR TAT.

Ting-a-Ling

1 King
Applies solely to the playing card.

2 Ring
A sometimes used allusion to an item of jewellery that has no vulgar associations. *See* PEARLY KING.

Tin Lid

Yid
An expression for a Jew that is often aimed at the Spurs supporter.

Tin Plate

Mate
Would appear to be a less well off rival to CHINA PLATE (qv) and is rarely used.

Tins of Beans

Jeans

An extension of BAKED BEANS (qv) that isn't often used but when it is it's in the cut down form of 'tins'.

Tin Tack(s)

1 Fact(s)
Gained popularity when BRASS TACKS (qv) stepped out of the boundaries of RS to join mainstream English.

2 Sack
A fairly common reference to dismissal from work.

Tin Tank

Bank
Sounds weaker and is inferior to IRON TANK (qv).

Tiny Tim

Flim (£5)
One of the many allusions to this sum of money. Based on the famous Dickensian gripple.

Tit For Tat

Hat
Always shortened to 'titfer', this is one of the few pieces of low speech to hit the heady heights of everyday language.

Tit Willow

Pillow
Based on an old song title this is a rarely used term but when it is it's never in a truncated form. It doesn't sound seemly to rest your head on a 'tit'.

To & Fro

Snow
A less vulgar alternative to COME & GO (qv).

Toby Jug(s)

1 Lug(s)
A reasonably well known example in relation to ears often the FA Cup handle type.

2 Mug
A very old piece relating to a fool and always clipped to a 'Toby'.

Tod Sloane

Alone
Extensively used in the first element, everyone likes to be 'one their Tod' once in a while. Based on the name of an American jockey who rode in Britain around the beginning of the century.

Toe Rag

Slag
In the early 60s this was 'boys' talk' for a girl of easy

virtue but later it evolved to mean an unpleasant person of either sex.

Toilet Roll　　*Dole*
May be wistfully employed by the long term unemployed when asked if he has found a job, 'No, still on the toilet.'

Tokyo Rose　　*Nose*
Named after a Japanese radio propaganda broadcaster of World War Two, this is generally cut to the first element, e.g., 'Why do you keep calling me Sinex?' 'Because you get right up my Tokyo.'

Tom Cat　　*Mat*
Usually a reference to a door mat on which to wipe your feet.

Tom & Dick　　*Sick*
A widely used piece that originally included the other member of the typical male trio, e.g., TOM HARRY & DICK (qv). Apart from the physical act of vomiting it applies to any form of illness of a not too serious nature. To be on the Tom and Dick is to be off work through ill health.

Tom & Jerry　　*Merry*
A reference to good natured inebriation this would appear to be based on the cartoon cat and mouse. But in the nineteenth century a Tom and Jerry was a low drinking house and *to* Tom and Jerry was to behave riotously.

Tomato Sauce　　*Horse*
Usually refers to a race horse, probably the one that is so far behind that it will never ketchup.

While we're on the subject of gee gees that run backwards this may be a good time to mention that in backslang horse becomes 'esroch'.

Tom Dooleys　　*Goolies (Testicles)*
Based on the eponymous hero of a song in reference to the spot where a kick may cause a man to hang down his head and cry.

Tomfoolery　　*Jewellery*
Mainly an underworld term that has been popularized by

numerous television crooks. Usually condensed to 'Tom' and often relates to 'knocked off gear going cheap'.

Tom, Harry & Dick *Sick*
Usually pared to 'Tom Harry' but *see* TOM & DICK.

Tom Mix *1 Fix*
In its original form this applies to being in a state of difficulty, i.e., 'to be in a right Tom Mix'. It has now slipped into the dirty world of drug abuse where a fix is an injection of a narcotic. Based on the name of a star of early western films (1880–1940).

2 Six
A common reference to £6 that is often employed as an alternative to its backslang counterpart 'exis'.

Tommy Dodd *1 God*
A very old example and used as 'Thank Tommy Dodd for that.' or 'Tommy Dodd knows.' A cemetery may be known as 'Tommy Dodd's garden'.

2 Odd
Can be employed in relation to strangeness and with a final 's' it refers to betting odds or the coin tossing opponent of MAJOR STEVENS (qv). In the mid 19th century a popular song contained the words 'Heads or tails are sure to win Tommy Dodd, Tommy Dodd'.

3 Rod (Gun)
This is an import from America but because of the dearth of weaponry terms it is included.

4 Sod
Can be used in times of difficulty or frustration. When the wife and kids are playing up it may be said, 'Tommy Dodd this for a game of mothers and fathers.'

Tommy Farr *Bar*
Named after a British heavyweight boxing champion in relation to where the drinks are served.

Tommy O'Rann *Scran*
An old piece of RS for an even older slang term for food or provisions.

Tommy Rollocks *Bollocks*

May be used either in reference to a great let down, i.e., A kick in the 'Tommys'. Or as an expression of disbelief, politely truncated to 'what a load of Tommy'. The term is never used in anger because the word is much more expressive and to the point.

Tommy Steel(s)   *Eel(s)*
Applies to that great cockney delicacy jellied eels and named after the London born entertainer.

Tommy Tripe   *Pipe*
Apart from that which is puffed at by the smoker, to pipe means to look at, e.g., 'Tommy the geezer in the Lionel Blairs, looks a right berk.'

Tommy Tucker   *Fucker*
An old term for a mischievous or spirited person. Normally said without malice.

Tommy Tupper   *Supper*
A fairly old reference to an evening food intake.

Tom Noddy   *Body*
Given that this example comes from the United States this probably alludes to a corpse. Tom Noddy is an old term for simpleton or fool.

Tom Thacker   *Tobacco*
An archaic piece that has probably burnt itself out in the ashtray of moribundity.

Tomorrow   *Borrow*
To be on the 'tomorrow' or the 'tom' usually means a small loan between friends or neighbours designed to be paid back the next day. But as we all know tomorrow never comes because when it does it's today again.

Tom Thumb   *Rum*
Possibly the term most likely to be used by rum drinkers as it refers to a tot.

Tom Tit(s)   *Shit(s)*
A very well known piece that actually means to defecate rather than the resultant mess, e.g., 'Cover for me while I go for a Tom Tit.' When pluralized it refers to diarrhoea.

Tom Tug   *Mug*
An old but rarely, if ever, used piece.

Tom Sawyer   *Lawyer*
May apply to those employed in the legal profession but often refers to the bar stool know-all whose freely given advice is seldom wanted or heeded. Based on a figment of Mark Twain's imagination.

Tooting Bec   *Peck*
A little kiss or a small bite to eat.

Top Hat   *Pratt*
Hard to believe that this word has become so acceptable, relating as it does to the vagina and to a fool in the same manner as cunt for which it is a variant. The term is never shortened and may be based on the annual upper class 'pose in' at Royal Ascot.

Touch & Tap   *Cap*
Both elements of the term are words meaning to borrow or cadge, which may be connected with going cap in hand for a hand-out.

Touched by the Moon   *Loon*
Once again a reference to a person with no top to his hat. Always reduced to 'a bit touched' which describes exactly what lunatic means. Not exactly RS but a good and apt expression.

Touch me on the Knob   *Bob*
An obviously obsolete example for a shilling (5p) that I have included because I would like to re-introduce an old phrase. To borrow money is to touch so the expression 'Can I touch you for a touch me?' used to be quite common. Much more colourful than 'five pee' don't you think?

Tower Bridge   *Fridge*
Always abridged to the first element, whereby cans of beer brought home from a party are referred to as prisoners and are 'bunged in the tower'.

Town Crier   *Liar*
Everybody knows a 'town crier', the person of whom you

disbelieve half of what he says and are dubious of the other half.

Town(s) & City(s)   *Tittie(s)*
An under developed variant of the famous BRISTOL CITY(S) (qv).

Treble Chance   *Dance*
Refers to a function and to what is possibly the biggest waste of energy man has ever devised.

T Rex   *Sex*
A predatory term from the would be sexual athlete. To go out on the pull is to be on the lookout for 'a bit of T Rex'. Named after a rock band of the early 70s.

Trick Cyclist   *Psychiatrist*
Not certain if this qualifies as RS but it is slang and it rhymes so here it is.

Trilby Hat   *Pratt*
Normally condensed to 'trilby' in regard to a fool.

Trolley & Tram   *Ham*
Generally sliced to the first of these two forerunners of the modern bus.

Trolley & Truck   *Fuck*
Used exclusively in reference to the sexual act.

Trombone   *Phone*
'The old trombone' is a fairly common expression.

Trouble & Fuss   *Bus*
Given the transport problems in London this is a very appropriate piece.

Trouble & Strife   *Wife*
By far the best known of all the terms for the woman who, in perfect circumstances, will be wooed, won and wed. On the other hand, she may be a case of bed, bun and brood.

Troubles & Cares   *Stairs*
A seldom climbed rival of APPLES & PEARS (qv).

Tug o' War

Whore
A lady who is often pulled.

Tumble & Trip

Whip
Chiefly reduced to a 'tumble' in relation to a collection or whip round.

Tumble Down the Sink

Drink
Always decreased to the first part and is principally connected with alcoholic drinks. To go for a 'tumble' is to go to the pub.

Turpentine

Serpentine
The lake in Hyde Park is known as 'the Turps' mainly by taxi drivers.

Turtle Dove(s)

1 Glove(s)
A well known piece that is always reduced to 'turtles'.

2 Love
An old term of romantic ballad writers in search of a rhyme.

Twelve Inch Rule

Fool
Yet another reference to a buffoon.

Twist & Twirl

Girl
Descriptive of what a young lady can do to a smitten swain. Round her little finger goes he.

Two & Eight

State
Nearly always termed as a 'right old two and eight' in reference to being on the horns of a dilemma.

Two Bob Bit(s)

Shit(s)
Most commonly applied in the plural form as an allusion to diarrhoea but may also refer to an emission of wind. In a malodorous atmosphere someone may ask through pinched nasal tones, 'Who's dropped a two bob bit?'

Two Foot Rule

Fool
An obsolete measure of stupidity, the predecessor to TWELVE INCH RULE (qv).

Two Thirty

Dirty

Refers to uncleanliness, e.g., 'His feet were so two thirty you could have grown potatoes on them.'

Typewriter

Fighter
Can apply to a boxer but mainly refers to strength of character. Anyone who keeps going through adversity is said to be 'a real typewriter'.

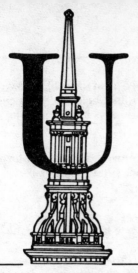

Ugly Sister   ***Blister***
That which painfully occurs on the hand after a bout of out of character tool usage or on the foot as a result of wearing a tight shoe or glass slipper.

Uncle & Aunt   ***Plant***
Refers to the growing kind rather than an industrial site.

Uncle Bert   ***Shirt***
An infrequent alternative to the famous DICKIE DIRT (qv). Sometimes used as Uncle Bertie for shirty meaning annoyed, e.g., 'What are you getting all Uncle Bertie about?'

Uncle Bob   ***Knob (Penis)***
Sometimes employed vulgarly by a less than smooth operator in the art of seduction, e.g., 'Come on darlin', come and meet my Uncle Bob.'

Uncle Dick   ***Sick***
Very common in relation to being physically sick or in general bad health. Often reduced to the second element as in 'dickie ticker'.

Uncle Fred   ***Bread***
A comical example whereby children are told 'Come on, eat your Uncle Fred.'

Uncle Mac   ***Smack***
Originally referred to a minor punishment but has since

cropped up in the malignant world of drug users as a term for heroin. Uncle Mac was a children's radio presenter in the early days of broadcasting.

Uncle Ned

Bed
This enjoys extensive employment usually in its full extension. Tired people can often hear their Uncle Ned calling.

Uncle Sam

Lamb
Applies to lamb as sold by the butcher.

Uncle Wilf

Filth (Police)
A recent example, used derogatorily.

Uncle Willie

1 Chilly
A general reference to coldness.

2 Silly
An allusion to a person acting in a manner that suggests sub standard mental equipment.

Union Jack

Back
Anatomically used, normally in relation to an aching back whereby an excuse for getting out of a strenuous job is 'I'm sorry I can't lift that, I've got a dodgy Union.'

Up & Down

Brown
Employed in reference to all things brown, most commonly ale.

Uriah Heep

Creep
An appropriate piece for the toady type inspired by the ever so 'umble Dickens character.

Vancouver　　*Hoover*
The brand name that has become synonymous with a vacuum cleaner.

Vanity Fair　　*Chair*
A very old example based on a very old book.

Vera Lynn　　*Gin*
Named after the songstress who won the hearts of the fighting men of World War Two, this is by far the commonest of all the terms for this spirit.

Veronica Lake　　*Steak*
The tastier alternative to JOE BLAKE (qv) based on the Hollywood star of the forties who was known as the Peek-a-boo girl (1919–73).

Vicar of Bray　　*Tray*
Applies either to the tool of the waiter's trade or to the number three for which tray is the parlyaree version.

Victoria Cross　　*Toss*
Used in an uncaring sense and abbreviated to 'I don't give a VC.'

Victoria Monk　　*Spunk (Semen)*
An example that stretches back to the days of music hall, of which Miss Monks was a star (1884–1972).

Vincent Price　　*Ice*
Frozen at 'Vincent' in respect of that which chills a drink. Aptly named after an American film star famed for his spine chilling roles.

Wait(s) & Linger(s)   *Finger(s)*
Points only in an anatomical direction.

Walter Joyce   *Voice*
An antiquated piece no longer heard.

Wanstead Flats   *Spats*
An obsolete term for a long departed fashion.

War & Strife   *Wife*
Another term rhyming the lady of the house with strife. I wonder why.

Warrior Bold   *Cold*
A reference to illness.

Watch & Chain   *Brain*
Often shortened to the timepiece part of the term in regard to either clever or dim folk. Of a dullard it may be said, 'His watch needs looking at,' or 'His watch is slow.' On the other hand a bright person's 'watch' may be fast. When castigating someone for not thinking it is generally used in full, e.g., 'Why don't you use your watch and chain once in a while?'

Waterloo   *Stew*
This is the dish and not a substitute for HOW D'YE DO (qv).

Weasel & Stoat   *Coat*

Common in the truncated form of 'weasel'.

Wee Georgie Wood *Good*
Named after a diminutive British comedian and generally shortened to 'Wee Georgie' as an alternative to ROBIN HOOD (qv).

Weekend Pass *Glass*
Probably a serviceman's term for a drinking receptacle.

Weep & Wail *Tale*
A particularly apposite piece for a sob story as told by a beggar.

Weeping Willow *Pillow*
An exhausted person may state, 'I'll be asleep as soon as my crust hits the weeping willow.'

Well Hung *Young*
Sounds like a woman's idea of the perfect toy boy.

West Ham Reserves *Nerves*
Used in terms of irritation or exasperation and condensed to, 'You're getting right on my West Hams, you really are.'

Westminster Abbey *Cabbie*
May be derived from the complaint of an American tourist that, 'Whatever journey I made in a London taxi I went past Westminster Abbey.' Actually it was a Japanese tourist but I can't type in Japanese.

Wheezy Anna *Spanner*
Formed on the name of an old comic song.

Whip & Lash *Tash (Moustache)*
Generally known as a 'whip'.

Whip & Top *Strop (Masturbate)*
Every schoolboy's dread is to be caught 'whipping' himself.

Whistle & Flute *Suit*
A supremely familiar piece that is always cut to a 'whistle'.

Whistle & Toot   *Loot (Money)*
Not heard much these days but 'toot' used to be fairly widespread.

Whitechapel   *Apple*
Named after an infamous area of East London renowned for murders, immigrants and the fruit and vegetable market at Spitalfields before it was transferred to Leyton E10 in 1991.

Wicked Rumours   *Bloomers*
A reference to ladies underwear, now used only in jest.

Widow's Mite   *Light*
A 'widow's' is a light for a cigarette or pipe.

Widow Twankey   *1 Hanky*
Decreased to the first element for a handkerchief.

2 Yankee
An American is known in some quarters as a 'widow'. Based on the pantomime character from Aladdin.

Wilbur Wright   *Flight*
A totally suitable example that is always trimmed to the Christian name of this pioneer of aviation, e.g., 'What time's your Wilbur?' Seems a bit unfair that Orville doesn't get a mention though. Wilbur lived from 1867 to 1912 and, for the sake of brotherly harmony, Orville from 1871 to 1948.

Wild West   *Vest*
A dated term for underwear.

Wilkie Bard(s)   *Card(s)*
Formed on the name of a music hall artiste this applies to any type of card. Wilkie was on the billboard of life from 1874 to 1944.

William Powell   *Towel*
Based on an American film star (1892–1984), this has its roots in prison.

William Tell   *Smell*
Applies to an odour of the obnoxious kind, e.g., 'It don't

half William Tell in here, somebody open a window.'

Will o' the Wisp(s) *Crisp(s)*
Crisps of any flavour, shape or texture are known as 'willers'.

Will's Whiff *Syph(ilis)*
A term that relates to any of the anti-social diseases. Based on a brand of cigar.

Wilson Pickett *Ticket*
Named after an American soul singer, this was valid in the 70s.

Windjammer *Hammer*
A tradesman's term.

Windsor Castle *Arse Hole*
The 'Brown Windsor' as it is known, is yet again the designated orifice up which the unwanted may be lodged. Also known as 'the queen's gaff'.

Wind Trap *Flap*
A flap is that piece of hair that semi-bald men pull from one side of the head to the other in a vain attempt to cover up the bare facts. This is a totally apt term because in breezy conditions the wind tends to get underneath the strategically placed locks causing them to behave in an unruly manner, often to be seen dancing like a demented squirrel's tail.

Win or Lose *Booze*
A racegoer's rhyme:
  Win or lose we have our booze
  But when we win we drink gin.

Wise Monkey *Dunkie (Condom)*
A most appropriate piece for a willie wellie, especially these days when the need for safe sex is paramount. A 'wise monkey' is therefore essential to deliver the old chap from evil. Also fitting that the number of wise monkeys corresponds with the traditional packet of three.

Wooden Plank *Yank*

A piece relating to our cousins over there especially when they are over here. During the Gulf War of 1991 taxi drivers were seen crying into their cocktails over 'the lack of wooden planks in town'.

Woolwich & Greenwich

Spinach
An alternative to CHARLTON & GREENWICH (qv) that has its roots in the greengrocery trade.

Woolwich Ferry

Sherry
A fairly common piece based on the Thames river crossing.

Working Class(es)

Glass(es)
Can apply either to a receptacle or to spectacles.

Worm(s) & Snail(s)

Nail(s)
A useful term to put kids off biting their fingernails which bears a resemblance to the warning, 'Don't bite your nails you'll get worms.'

Worry & Strife

Wife
An infrequent but an equally apposite variant of TROUBLE & STRIFE (qv).

Wyatt Earp

Burp
Some ignoramuses think it hilarious to burp at a high rate of decibels. Such people are sometimes nicknamed 'Wyatt'. Based on the legendary American lawman who may or may not have suffered with indigestion. Born in 1848 he reputably survived many gunfights including the famous one against the Clantons at the OK Corral in 1881. He died in 1929.

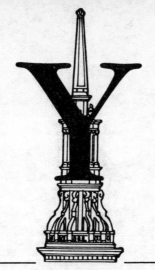

Yard of Tripe   *Pipe*
Not exactly an ad-man's dream of a term. 'Live in peace with your yard of tripe'? I don't think so.

Yarmouth Bloater   *Motor*
A piece that harks back to the days when only the toffs had cars.

Yorkshire Rippers   *Slippers*
A fairly recent example based on the media nickname for the mass murderer Peter Sutcliffe.

Yorkshire Tyke   *Mike (Microphone)*
A term that had its formation in the entertainment business and was taken up by those doing a turn down the pub. Not been heard of for a while but may be on the verge of a comeback given the present karaoke craze.

You & Me   *Tea*
An elderly piece that is still on the boil.

Yours & Ours   *Flowers*
An example that was grown by florists.

Yuletide Log(s)   *Dog(s)*
An alternative to CHRISTMAS LOG (qv) in reference to greyhounds. Both these terms are left in the traps by CHERRY HOG (qv).

Zachary Scotts   *Trots*
Named after an American movie star (1914–65), the 'Zacharys' is a reference to diarrhoea.

Zasu Pitts   *Shits*
And another term for the squitters courtesy of Hollywood. Miss Pitts was an actress of many films.

Zorba the Greek   *Leak (Urinate)*
Based on the name of a popular film, this is always known as a 'Zorba'.

Reverse Dick'n'arry

Actor	Max Factor	**Bald**	Cyril Lord
Advice	Lump of Ice		Oh My God
Ale	Daily Mail	**Balls (Testicles)**	
All right	Shiny & Bright		Cobbler's Awls
Alone	Darby & Joan		Cobbler's Stalls
	Jack Jones		Coffee Stalls
	Jack Malone		Marble Halls
	Pat Malone		Max Walls
	Tod Sloane		Niagara Falls
Ancestors	Aunt's Sisters		Nobby Halls
Apple	Whitechapel		Orchestra Stalls
Arc (Light)	Finsbury Park		Sammy Halls
Arm(s)	False Alarm(s)	**Banana**	Gertie Gitana
Arms	Chalk Farms	**Banger**	Bernhard Langer
	Fire Alarms		Coat Hanger
Army	Daft & Barmy		Doppelganger
	Kate Karney	**Bank**	Chain & Crank
Arse	Bottle & Glass		Iron Tank
	By Pass		J Arthur Rank
	Khyber Pass		Tin Tank
Arse Hole	Elephant & Castle	**Bar**	Bazaar
	Windsor Castle		Jack Tar
Aunt	Garden Plant		Near & Far
	Mrs Chant		There You Are
Baby	Basin of Gravy		Tommy Farr
Bacardi	Kiss Me Hardy	**Barber**	Dover Harbour
	Laurel & Hardy	**Barge**	Davy Large
Back	Cilla Black	**Barmy**	Dad's Army
	Hammer & Tack		Lakes of Killarny
	Haystack		Salvation Army
	Penny Black	**Barrow**	Cock Sparrow
	Union Jack	**Basin**	Charlie Mason
Bad	Jack the Lad		Jimmy Mason
	Sorry & Sad	**Bat**	This & That
Bag(s)	Harry Tagg(s)	**Bath**	Hat & Scarf
Bail	Holy Nail	**Beak (Magistrate)**	
	Royal Mail		Bubble & Squeak
Baker	Long Acre		Once A Week
		Bean(s)	King(s) & Queen(s)

Beano	Dan Leno	**Bird**	Lemon Curd
Beard	Just as I Feared		Richard the Third
	Strangely Weird	**Bitter (Ale)**	Apple Fritter
Bed	Roses Red		Diesel Fitter
	Uncle Ned		Gary Glitter
Beef	Stop Thief		Giggle & Titter
Beer	Christmas Cheer		Tex Ritter
	Crimea	**Black**	Coalman's Sack
	Far & Near		Jumping Jack
	Fusilier	**Blade**	First Aid
	Never Fear		Shovel & Spade
	Oh My Dear	**Blind**	All Behind
	Pig's Ear		Golden Hind
Beetle(s)	Pin(s) & Needle(s)	**Blister**	Ugly Sister
Belch	Raquel Welch	**Bloke**	Bushel of Coke
Believe	Christmas Eve		Heap of Coke
Bell	Little Nell		Lump of Coke
Belly	Auntie Nellie	**Blood**	Roy Hudd
	Derby Kelly	**Bloomers**	Montezumas
	George Melly		Wicked Rumours
	Ned Kelly	**Blow**	Rotten Row
	New Delhi	**Blower**	Percy Thrower
Ben (Truman)		**Blowy**	David Bowie
	Jenny Wren	**Blue**	Danny La Rue
	Never Again		Irish Stew
Bent	Duke of Kent	**Boat**	Frog in the Throat
	Stoke on Trent		Hat & Coat
Berk	Charlie Smirke		I'm Afloat
Best	Pants & Vest		Nanny Goat
Bet	National Debt	**Bob**	Kettle on the Hob
Big	Porky Pig		One for His Nob
Big 'un	Barry McGuigan		Touch Me on the Knob
Bike	Clever Mike	**Bodgers**	Roy Rogers
	Dirty Tyke	**Body**	Big Ears & Noddy
	Pat & Mike		Hot Toddy
Bill	Beechams Pill		Tom Noddy
	Jack & Jill	**Bog**	Cat & Dog
	Pitch & Fill		Kermit the Frog
Bingo	George & Ringo	**Bogie (Nasal Residue)**	
Bins	Errol Flynns		Jimmy Logie

Boil	Can of Oil	**Boy Scout**	Brussels Sprout
	Conan Doyle		Tea Grout
Bollocks	Castor & Pollux	**Braces**	Epsom Races
	Fun & Frolics	**Brain**	Watch & Chain
	Johnny Rollocks	**Brake(s)**	Francis Drake(s)
	Tommy Rollocks	**Brandy**	Charlie Randy
Bombs	Derry & Toms		Fine & Dandy
Bone(s)	Stick(s) & Stone(s)		Jack-A-Dandy
			Sugar Candy

Bonkers (Mad)
Marbles & Conkers

Brass (Money)
Beggar Boy's Arse

Book	Captain Hook	**Brat**	Jack Sprat
	Jackdaw & Rook	**Bread**	Needle & Thread
	Rookery Nook		Strike Me Dead
Boot(s)	German Flute(s)		Uncle Fred
	King Canute(s)	**Breath**	King Death
	Daisy Roots		Life & Death
Booze	Pick & Choose	**Brick**	Clever Dick
	River Ouse		King Dick
	Win or Lose	**Brickie**	Clever Dickie
Boozer	Battle Cruiser		King Dickie
	Cabin Cruiser	**Bride**	Fat & Wide
Borders	Harry Lauders		Mother's Pride
Bore	Man o' War	**Broke**	Coal(s) & Coke
Boring	Snoozing & Snoring		Hearts of Oak
Born	Got out of Pawn	**Brokers**	Engineers & Stokers
Borrow	Tomorrow	**Broom**	Bride & Groom
Boss	Dead Loss	**Brother**	Manhole Cover
	Joe Goss		One & T'other
	Pitch & Toss	**Brown**	Camden Town
Bottle	Aristotle		Half a Crown

Bounce (Cheat)
Half Ounce

			Kentish Town
Bouncer	Half Ouncer		Up & Down

Bowler (Hat)
Steamroller

		Bruise	Evening News
Box	Artful Fox	**Brush**	Blackbird & Thrush
	Nervo & Knox		Ian Rush
Boy	Hobber de Hoy		Song of the Thrush
	Pride & Joy	**Bucket**	Mrs Duckett
	Saveloy		Nantucket
	San Toy(s)	**Bug**	Steam Tug

Bum	Big Brass Drum		La-Di-Da
	Deaf & Dumb	**Card**	Bladder of Lard
	Fife & Drum		Prussian Guard
	Pipe & Drum		Six Months Hard
Bunce	D for Dunce	**Card(s)**	Wilkie Bard(s)
Bung	Jimmy Young		Coldstream Guards
Bunion	Spanish Onion		Feet & Yards
Bunk	Pineapple Chunk	**Carriage**	Love & Marriage
Burp	Wyatt Earp	**Carrot**	Polly Parrot
Burton (Beer)		**Carzey (Lavatory)**	
	Lace Curtain		Benghazi
Bus	Swear & Cuss	**Case**	Bootlace
	Trouble & Fuss		Crowded Space
Business	Bees Knees		Faraway Place
Butter	Cough & Splutter	**Cash**	Arthur Ashe
	Mumble & Mutter		Henry Nash
	Roll me in the Gutter		Knotty Ash
	Stammer & Stutter		Oak & Ash
Button	Leg of Mutton		Oscar Asche
	Len Hutton		Pie & Mash
			Sausage & Mash
Cab	Flounder & Dab	**Cat**	Ball of Fat
	Sandy McNab		Brown Hat
	Smash & Grab	**Ceiling**	Funny Feeling
Cabbage	Joe Savage	**Cell**	Flowery Dell
Cabbie	Westminster Abbey	**Celluloid**	Harold Lloyd
Cadge	Coat & Badge	**Chain**	Frankie Laine
	Doggett's Coat &	**Chair**	Burke & Hare
	Badge		Here & There
Cake	Give & Take		Lionel Blair
	Put & Take		Lion's Lair
	Sexton Blake		Lion's Share
	Swan Lake		Vanity Fare
Can	Charlie Chan	**Chairs**	Owen Nares
Candle	Harry Randall	**Chalk**	Careless Talk
	Jack Randle		Lambeth Walk
Cap	Game of Nap	**Change**	Kitchen Range
	Touch & Tap		Rifle Range
Caper (Game)		**Char (Tea)**	There You Are
	Brown Paper	**Charlie**	Oats & Barley
Car	Jam Jar	**Cheek**	Hide & Seek

	Once A Week		Horse & Trap
Cheers	Big Ears	**Claret**	Boiled Beef & Carrot
Cheese	Balmy Breeze		Eighteen Carat
	Bended Knees	**Cleaner**	Auntie Ena
	Cough & Sneeze		Semolina
	Evening Breeze	**Clock**	Blackpool Rock
	Stand at Ease		Dickory Dock
Cheeser	Julius Caesar		Postman's Knock
Cheque	Duchess of Teck	**Clothes**	These & Those
	Duke of Teck	**Cloudy**	Dull & Doudy
	Goose's Neck	**Clown**	Charlie Brown
	Gregory Peck	**Club**	Rub-a-Dub-Dub
	Pain in the Neck	**Clutch**	Lord Sutch
Chest	Bird's Nest	**Coach**	Cockroach
	East & West	**Coal**	Merry Old Soul
	Mae West	**Coat**	Bucket Afloat
Chicken	Charlie Dicken		I'm Afloat
Chief	Bully Beef		John O'Groat
	Ham & Beef		Pound Note
	Joint of Beef		Quaker Oat
	Plate of Beef		Weasel & Stoat
Chill	Frock & Frill		
Chilly	Uncle Willy	**Cock (Penis)**	
Chin	Errol Flynn		Almond Rock
	Gunga Din		Brighton Rock
	Thick & Thin		Dickory Dock
Chink	Tiddly Wink		Grandfather Clock
Chip(s)	Lucky Dip(s)		Stick of Rock
Chopper (Penis)		**Cocoa**	Orinoko
	Gobstopper	**Cod**	Richard Todd
Church	Chicken Perch	**Cods (Testicles)**	
	Lean & Lurch		Ken Dodds
	Left in the Lurch	**Coffee**	Everton Toffee
Cider	Runner & Rider	**Coke**	Holy Smoke
Cigar	Bucks Hussar	**Cold**	Brave & Bold
	La-Di-Da		Naughton & Gold
	Spanish Guitar		Potatoes in the Mould
Cinder(s)	Polly Flinder(s)		Soldier Bold
Clanger (Mistake)			Warrior Bold
	Penny Banger	**Collar**	Half a Dollar
Clap (VD)	Handicap		Hollar Boys Hollar
			Shout & Hollar

Collar & Tie	Swallow & Sigh	**Cramp**	Rising Damp
Comb	Garden Gnome	**Crap**	Game of Nap
	Ideal Home		Horse & Trap
Come	Pedigree Chum		Pony & Trap
Conk (Nose)		**Crash/Smash**	
	Glass of Plonk		Jack Flash
Cook	Babbling Brook		Sausage & Mash
Coon	Cameroon	**Crazy**	Buttercup & Daisy
	Egg & Spoon	**Creep**	Uriah Heep
	Harvest Moon	**Cripple**	Strawberry Ripple
	Macaroon	**Crisp(s)**	Will o' the Wisp(s)
	Silvery Moon	**Crook**	Babbling Brook
Cop (Policeman)			Joe Hook
	Bottle Top		Joe Rook
	Ginger Pop	**Cross (Angry)**	
Cop(s)	Lollipop(s)		Milkman's Horse
	Pork Chop(s)	**Crutch (Crotch)**	
Copper	Bottle & Stopper		Lord Sutch
	Clod Hopper		Rabbit Hutch
	Grasshopper	**Cry**	Drip Dry
Cords	House of Lords		Pipe Your Eye
Cork	Duke of York		Snoop & Pry
Corn	Cape Horn	**Cuddle**	Mix & Muddle
Corner	Jack Horner	**Cue**	Black & Blue
	Johnny Horner	**Cunt**	Berkshire Hunt
Cory (Penis)			Charlie Hunt
	Gruesome & Gory		Eyes Front
	Morning Glory		Grannie Grunt
Cot	Flower Pot		Groan & Grunt
Cough	Horse & Trough		Grumble & Grunt
Course	Iron Horse		Joe Hunt
Cousin	Baker's Dozen		National Front
Cow	Ruck & Row		Sharp & Blunt
Coward	Charlie Howard		Sir Anthony Blunt
	Frankie Howerd	**Cup**	Dog & Pup
Crab(s) (Crab Lice)		**Cupboard**	Mother Hubbard
	Beattie & Babs	**Curry**	Ruby Murray
	Dribs & Drabs	**Curtain(s)**	Richard Burton(s)
	Sandy McNabs	**Cut**	Fruit & Nut
	Taxi Cab(s)		
		Dance	South of France

	Treble Chance		London Fog
Danger	Lone Ranger	**Dog(s)**	Yuletide Log(s)
	Stewart Grainger	**Dog & Duck (Pub)**	
Dark	Noah's Ark		Snog & Fuck
Darts	Horse & Carts	**Dole**	Cob of Coal
Daughter	Bricks & Mortar		Jam Roll
	Holy Water		Nat King Cole
	Soap & Water		Old King Cole
Day	Blue & Grey		Rock'n'Roll
Dead	Brown Bread		Toilet Roll
	Gone to Bed	**Dollar**	Oxford Scholar
Deaf	Mutt & Jeff		Shirt & Collar
Deaner (5p)		**Done**	Hit & Run
	Riverina	**Door**	George Bernard Shaw
Deuce	Bottle of Spruce		Rory O'More
Devil	Henry Meville	**Dope**	Bar of Soap
Diamond	Simple Simon		Bob Hope
Diary	Kilburn Priory		Joe Soap
Dice	Block of Ice	**Double**	Rasher & Bubble
	Choc Ice	**Dozen**	Country Cousin
	Rats & Mice	**Draft**	George Raft
Dictionary	Dick'n'arry	**Drag**	Carpet Bag
Die	Say Goodbye	**Dragon**	Covered Wagon
Diesel	Board & Easel	**Drain**	Spanish Main
	Pop Goes the Weasel	**Draught**	George Raft
Diet	Peace & Quiet	**Drawers**	Diana Dors
Diggins	Charlie Wiggins		Early Doors
Digs (Lodgings)		**Dream**	Custard Cream
	Ronnie Biggs	**Dress**	Daily Express
Dinner	Jim Skinner		More or Less
	Lilley & Skinner	**Drink**	Tiddly Wink
	Saint & Sinner		Tumble Down the
Dirty	Two Thirty		Sink
Dive	Beehive	**Dripping**	Dr Crippen
Do So	Robinson Crusoe	**Drop**	Lollipop
Doctor	King's Proctor	**Drum**	Finger & Thumb
Dog	Cherry Hog	**Drunk**	Elephant's Trunk
	Christmas Log		Jumbo's Trunk
	Golliwog		Salt Junk

Dumb	Red Rum		Spit & Drag
Dunkie (Condom)		**Fairy**	Canary
	Brass Monkey	**Fake**	Corn Flake
	Wise Monkey		Kidstake
Dyke	Raleigh Bike		Sexton Blake
		Fan	Frying Pan
Ear	Bottle of Beer		Mary Ann
	Glass of Beer	**Fanny**	Jack & Danny
	King Lear	**Fare**	Grey Mare
Ear(s)	Fusilier(s)	**Fart**	Apple Tart
	Southend Pier(s)		Billy Smart
Eat	Tidy & Neat		D'Oyly Carte
Eel(s)	John Peel(s)		Horse & Cart
	Tommy Steel(s)		Raspberry Tart
Egg	Arm & Leg	**Farted**	Chicken Hearted
	Borrow & Beg	**Fat**	Jack Sprat
	Tent Peg	**Father**	Soap & Lather
Eight	Garden Gate	**Feet**	Plates of Meat
	Harry Tate		Platter of Meat
Erection	General Election	**Fiddle**	Hi Diddle Diddle
Evens	Major Stevens		Nelson Riddle
Eye	Mutton Pie	**Fight**	Dynamite
	Steak & Kidney Pie		Left & Right
Eye(s)	Mince Pies		Read & Write
	Pudding(s) & Pie(s)	**Fighter**	Typewriter
		File	Duke of Argyll
Face	Boat Race		Plymouth Argyll
	Chevy Chase	**Filth (Police)**	
	Deuce & Ace		Uncle Wilf
	Fillet of Plaice	**Fin**	Lincoln's Inn
	Glass Case	**Finger**	Lean & Linger
	Jem Mace	**Finger(s)**	Long(s) & Linger(s)
	Kipper & Plaice		Wait(s) & Linger(s)
	Roach & Dace	**Finn**	Lincoln's Inn
Fact	Brass Tack	**Fire**	Anna Maria
	Tic Tac		Ave Maria
Fact(s)	Tin Tack(s)		Black Maria
Fag	Cough & Drag		Jeremiah
	Harry Wragg		Obadiah
	Oily Rag	**Fish**	Andy McNish
	Old Nag		
	Puff & Drag		

	Lillian Gish
Fist	Oliver Twist
Five	Beehive
	Jacks Alive
	Man Alive
Fiver (£5)	Deep Sea Diver
	Lady Godiva
	Sky Diver
Fix	Seven & Six
	Tom Mix
Flag	Castle Rag
	Old Rag
Flap	Wind Trap
Flares	Grosvenor Squares
	Lionel Blairs
Flea	Bonny Dundee
	Jenny Lee
	Nancy Lea
Flicks	Box of Tricks
Flight	Wilbur Wright
Flim (£5)	Tiny Tim
Floor	Mrs More
	Rory O'More
Floored	Mogadored
Flower(s)	April Showers
	Early Hour(s)
	Happy Hour(s)
Flowers	Yours & Ours
Flu	Lousy Lou
	Scraggy Lou
Fluke	Iron Duke
Flutter (Bet)	
	Grumble & Mutter
Fly	Meat Pie
	Nelly Bligh
Flying Squad	
	Sweeney Todd
Food	Don't Be Rude
	In the Mood
	In the Nude

Fool	Lump of School
	Twelve Inch Rule
	Two Foot Rule
Foot	Chimney & Soot
Football Pools	
	April Fools
Foreman	Bill O'Gorman
Fork	Duke of York
	Joe Rourke
	Roast Pork
Four	Dirty Whore
	Knocker on the Door
Free	Buckshee
Freezer	Julius Caesar
	Mona Lisa
French	Muddy Trench
Fridge	Tower Bridge
Friend	Mile End
Frog	Jiggle & Jog
Front	James Hunt
	National Front
Fuck	Aylesbury Duck
	Cattle Truck
	Donald Duck
	Flying Duck
	Friar Tuck
	Goose & Duck
	Push in the Truck
	Rubber Duck
	Russian Duck
	Trolley & Truck
Fucker	Feather Plucker
	Pheasant Plucker
	Tommy Tucker
Fuck It	Mop & Bucket
	Mrs Duckett
Full	John Bull
Gallon	Flanagan & Allen
Gam (Fellatio)	
	Plate of Ham

	Slice of Ham
Garage	Horse & Carriage
Garden	Beg Your Pardon
	Dolly Varden
Gay (Homosexual)	
	Darling Buds of May
	Doris Day
Geezer	Ice Cream Freezer
	Lemon Squeezer
Ghost	Pillar & Post
	Slice of Toast
Gin	Brain O'Linn
	Bung It In
	Father O'Flynn
	Lincoln's Inn
	Mother's Ruin
	Needle & Pin
	Nell Gwynne
	Ralph Lynn
	Thick & Thin
	Vera Lynn
Girl	Mother of Pearl
	Ribbon & Curl
	Twist & Twirl
Glass	Weekend Pass
Glass(es)	Hackney Marsh(es)
	Working Class(es)
Glasses	Mountain Passes
Glove(s)	Turtle Dove(s)
Glue	Mary Lou
Go	Scapa Flow
Gob (Phlegm)	
	Couple o' Bob
God	Tommy Dodd
Going	Swiftly Flowing
Gold	Hot & Cold
Good	Wee Georgie Wood
Good(s)	Robin Hood(s)
Gout	Salmon & Trout
Graft	George Raft

Grass (Informant)	
	Duck's Arse
Grass	Old Iron & Brass
Gravy	Army & Navy
	Royal Navy
Greek	Bubble & Squeak
Green(s)	Nellie Dean(s)
Greens	God Save the Queens
	Has Beens
Grey	Night & Day
Groom	Skinny as a Broom
Ground	Penny a Pound
	Safe & Sound
Guards	Christmas Cards
Guest	Georgie Best
Gums	Breadcrumbs
	Currants & Plums
Gun	Hot Cross Bun
Gut	Limehouse Cut
Guts	Newington Butts
Gutter	Bread & Butter
Haddock	Bessie Braddock
	Fanny Craddock
Hag	Old Bag
Hair	Barnet Fair
	Fanny Blair
	Fred Astaire
Half	Cows & Calf
	Shower Bath
Ham	Hop it & Scram
	Trolley & Tram
Hammer	Stutter & Stammer
	Windjammer
Hand	Frying Pan
	Martin-le-Grand
	Brass Bands
	Darby Bands
	German Band(s)
	Margate Sand(s)

	Ramsgate Sand(s)		Flake of Corn
	St Martin-le-Grand(s)		Mountains of Mourne
Handle	Harry Randle		Popcorn
Handy	Sugar Candy		Sunday Morn
Hanky	Widow Twankey	**Horse**	Apple Sauce
			Bottle of Sauce
Hanky Panky (Deception)			Charing Cross
	Moody & Sankey		Tomato Sauce
Hard	Bread & Lard	**Hospital**	Horse Piddle
Harm	Chalk Farm	**Hot**	Captain Scott
Hat	Ball & Bat		Flower Pot
	This & That		Peas in the Pot
	Tit for Tat	**House**	Cat & Mouse
Head	Ball of Lead		Flea & Louse
	Crust of Bread		Mickey Mouse
	Loaf of Bread		Rat & Mouse
	Lump of Lead		
	Penn'orth of Bread	**Ice**	Fleas & Lice
Heart	D'Oyly Carte		Sugar & Spice
	Jam Tart		Vincent Price
	Raspberry Tart	**Immigrant**	Jimmy Grant
	Stop & Start	**Ink**	Herman Fink
	Strawberry Tart	**Iron (Hoof) (Homosexual)**	
Heater	Blue Peter		Lenny the Lion
Heaven	Cloud Seven	**Itch(y)**	Little Tich(y)
Hell	Bucket & Well		
	Daisy Bell	**Jacket**	Fag Packet
	Ding Dong Bell		Tennis Racket
Hill	Jack & Jill	**Jail**	Bucket & Pail
Hole	Merry Old Soul		Ginger Ale
	Rock 'n' Roll		Jug & Pail
			Sorrowful Tale
Hole (Anus)		**Jam**	Amsterdam
	North Pole	**Jap**	Rat Trap
	South Pole	**Jaw**	Jackdaw
Home	Gates of Rome	**Jaxie (Anus)**	
	Pope of Rome		London Taxi
Homo	Perry Como	**Jazz**	Razzmatazz
Hooter	Pea-shooter	**Jeans**	Baked Beans
Hoover	Vancouver		String Beans
Horn (Erection)			Tins of Beans
	Colleen Bawn		
	Early Morn		

Jelly	Mother Kelly		Kerry Packer(s)
Jerry	Fred Perry	**Knee(s)**	Robert E Lee
Jew	Buckle My Shoe	**Knees**	Birds & Bees
	Fifteen Two		Biscuits & Cheese
	Five To Two	**Knickers**	Bill Stickers
	Four by Two	**Knife**	Charming Wife
	Half Past Two		Darling Wife
	Kangaroo		Drum & Fife
	Pot of Glue		Duke of Fife
	Quarter Past Two		Husband and Wife
	Quarter To Two		Man & Wife
	Tea For Two		
	Ten To Two	**Knob (Penis)**	
Jewellery	Tomfoolery		Uncle Bob
Job	Couple o' Bob	**Knocker**	Davy Jones's Locker
	Knocker & Knob		Mozzle & Brocha
Jock (Scot)	Sweaty Sock	**Knockers (Bosoms)**	
Johnny (Condom)			Mods & Rockers
	Reggie & Ronnie	**Kraut (German)**	
Joker	Tapioca		Holler & Shout
Judge	Barnaby Rudge		Luger Lout
	Chocolate Fudge	**Labour**	Beggar my Neighbour
	Inky Smudge	**Lace(s)**	Funny Face(s)
Kettle	Hansel & Gretel	**Ladder**	Blackadder
	Scrap Metal		Leaky Bladder
Key(s)	Jenny Lee	**Lager**	Forsyte Saga
	Housemaid's Knee(s)	**Lamb**	Uncle Sam
	Knobbly Knee(s)	**Lark**	Bushy Park
Kid(s)	Dustbin Lid		Joan of Arc
	Saucepan Lid	**Last**	Damn & Blast
	Tea Pot Lid	**Late**	Tiddler's Bait
	God Forbid	**Later**	Alligator
King	Gold Ring	**Laugh**	Cow & Calf
	Ting-a-Ling	**Lavatory**	Family Tree
Kip (Sleep)	Feather & Flip	**Lawyer**	Tom Sawyer
	Halfpenny Dip	**Lazy**	Gert & Daisy
	Jockey's Whip	**Lead (Dog's Leash)**	
Kipper	Jack the Ripper		Beryl Reid
Kiss	Hit & Miss	**Leak (Urinate)**	
Knacker(s)	Christmas Cracker		Zorba the Greek
	Cream Crackers		

Leather	Tar & Feather		Touched by the Moon
Leave	Bob & Weave	**Loony**	Mickey Rooney
Leg(s)	Bacon & Eggs	**Loot (Money)**	
	Clothes Pegs		Whistle & Toot
	Cribbage Peg	**Lorry**	Sad & Sorry
	Dutch Peg(s)	**Lost**	Jack Frost
	Ham & Egg(s)	**Lot**	Hopping Pot
	Nutmeg(s)	**Louse**	Rat & Mouse
	Scotch Egg(s)	**Lousy**	Housey Housey
	Scotch Peg(s)		
	Scrambled Egg(s)	**Love**	Heavens Above
Level	Red Devil		Turtle Dove
Liar	Dunlop Tyre	**Luck**	Donald Duck
	Holy Friar	**Lug(s)**	Toby Jug(s)
	Town Crier	**Lunch**	Judy & Punch
Lid (Hat)	God Forbid		Kidney Punch
Lie	Collar & Tie	**Lush**	Comb & Brush
Lie(s)	Pork Pie(s)		
Life	Fork & Knife	**Mad**	Mum & Dad
	Struggle & Strife	**Magistrate**	Garden Gate
Light	Widow's Mite	**Maid**	Bucket & Spade
Light (Ale)	Chalky White	**Man**	Pot & Pan
	Day & Night	**Marge**	Little & Large
	Silent Night	**Mark**	Hyde Park
	Stage Fright	**Married**	Cut & Carried
Light (Illumination)		**Marry**	Cash & Carry
	Day & Night		Dot & Carry
Light(s)	Merry & Bright(s)	**Mat**	Dog & Cat
Line	Grape Vine		Tom Cat
Lip(s)	Apple Pips	**Match**	Itch & Scratch
	Battleship	**Matches**	Bites & Scratches
	Fish & Chip(s)		Cuts & Scratches
	PG Tips	**Mate**	China Plate
Liver	Bow & Quiver		Harry Tate
	Swanee River		Tin Plate
Lodger	Artful Dodger	**Meat**	Hands & Feet
	Jolly Roger	**Melons (Breasts)**	
Look	Butcher's Hook		Mary Ellens
Loon	Full Moon	**Memory**	Dick Emery
	Keith Moon		
	Man in the Moon		

Mental	Radio Rental
Menu	Me & You
Merry	Tom & Jerry
Meter	Little Peter
Mick	Shovel & Pick
Middle	Hi Diddle Diddle
Mike (Microphone)	Yorkshire Tyke
Mild (Ale)	Marty Wilde
	Oscar Wilde
Milk	Charlie Dilke
	Satin & Silk
Minder	Organ Grinder
Minute	Cock Linnet
Missus	Hugs & Kisses
	Love & Kisses
	Plates & Dishes
Moan	Darby & Joan
Mole	Nat King Cole
Moll	Paper Doll
Money	Bees & Honey
	Bread & Honey
	Bugs Bunny
	Pot of Honey
	Sugar & Honey
Moody	Punch & Judy
Moon	Silver Spoon
Morning	Days a Dawning
	Gypsy's Warning
Mother	God Love Her
	One & T'Other
Motor	Kipper & Bloater
	Tea for Two and a
	Bloater
	Yarmouth Bloater
Mouse	Maxwell House
Mouth	North & South
	Queen of the South
	Sunny South
Muddle	Kiss & Cuddle

Mug	Barge & Tug
	Steam Tug
	Toby Jug
	Tom Tug
Muggins (Idiot)	Harry Huggins
Mum	Finger & Thumb
Muscle(s)	Green(s) & Brussel(s)
Mussel	Jane Russell
Mutton	Billy Button
Nag	Flea Bag
	Paper Bag
Nail	Daily Mail
Nail(s)	Slug(s) & Snail(s)
	Monkey's Tail(s)
	Worm(s) & Snail(s)
Nancy (Homosexual)	Tickle Your Fancy
Nap	Mouse Trap
Nark (Informer)	Car Park
	Grass in the Park
	Hyde Park
	Noah's Ark
Navy	Lumpy Gravy
	Plain & Gravy
	Pudding & Gravy
	Soup & Gravy
Neck	Bushel & Peck
	Gregory Peck
Needle	Jeremy Beadle
Neighbour	Hard Labour
News	Bottle of Booze
Nice	Apples & Rice
	Sugar & Spice
Nick	Cow's Lick
	Dirty Dick
	Moby Dick
	Shovel & Pick
Nicker (£1)	Eels & Liquor

Niece	Bit & Piece		Molly O'Morgan
Nigger	Grave Digger	**Over**	Chatham & Dover
	Mechanical Digger		
	Square Rigger	**Paddock**	Smoked Haddock
Night	Black & White	**Paddy**	Goodie & Baddie
Nine	Feel Fine	**Pain**	Hangar Lane
	Mother of Mine		Kennington Lane
Nip (Japanese)			Michael Caine
	Micro Chip		Petticoat Lane
	Orange Pip	**Paki**	Flunkey & Lackey
Nipple(s)	Raspberry Ripple(s)		Half Ounce of Baccy
Nippy	George & Zippy		Ounce of Baccy
No	Brown Joe	**Pan**	Isle of Man
Noise	Box of Toys	**Panel**	English Channel
	Girls & Boys		Soap & Flannel
	Theydon Bois	**Pants**	Beetles & Ants
Nose	Fireman's Hose		Insects & Ants
	I Suppose	**Paper**	Linen Draper
	Ruby Rose		Skyscraper
	Tokyo Rose	**Parcel**	Elephant & Castle
Nosh	Mouthwash	**Pardon**	Covent Garden
Nerves	West Ham Reserves	**Park**	Joan of Ark
Nude	Dirty & Rude		Light & Dark
Number	Cucumber		Skylark
Nuts (Fruit)	Fat Guts	**Parole**	Jam Role
Nuts (Testicles)		**Party**	Hale & Hearty
	Comic Cuts		Moriarty
	General Smuts		Russell Harty
Nutter	Bread & Butter	**Pass**	Old Iron & Brass
		Path	Oats & Chaff
Oak	Plymouth Cloak	**Pawn**	Bullock's Horn
Oats (Sexual Satisfaction)		**Pear**	Teddy Bear
	John O'Groats	**Peck**	Tooting Bec
Odd	Tommy Dodd	**Pee/Wee**	Cup of Tea
Oil	Ruin & Spoil		Fiddle De Dee
One	Penny Bun		Fiddlers Three
Onions	Corns & Bunions		Jerry Lee
Orders	Harry Lauders		Riddle-me-ree
Organ	Captain Morgan		Southend-on-Sea
		Pen	Bill & Ben

	Cock & Hen		Weeping Willow
	Dirty Den	**Pills (Testicles)**	
Penis	Good Ship Venus		Barnacle Bills
	Mars & Venus	**Pimp**	Mac Gimp
Penny	Jack Benny	**Pinch**	Half Inch
	Kilkenny	**Pink**	Rinky Dink
	Abergavenny	**Pint of Ale**	Ship in Full Sail
Pension	Stand to Attention	**Pipe**	Cherry Ripe
Pepper	Dirty Leper		Tommy Tripe
	High Stepper		Yard of Tripe
Pest	Bird's Nest	**Piss**	Arthur Bliss
	Georgie Best		Boo & Hiss
Phone	Eau de Cologne		Cuddle & Kiss
	Darby & Joan		French Kiss
	Dog & Bone		Goodnight Kiss
	Ham-bone		Hit & Miss
	Mike Malone		Micky Bliss
	Molly Malone		Snakes Hiss
	Trombone		Ta Ta Kiss
Photo	Kipper & Bloater		That & This
Piano	Joanna	**Pissed (Drunk)**	
Pickle	Slap & Tickle		Brahms & Liszt
Pickle(s)	Harvey Nichol(s)		Fog & Mist
Piddle	Dicky Diddle		Hand & Fist
	Jimmy Riddle		Mozart & Liszt
	Pig in the Middle		Scotch Mist
Pie	Black Eye	**Pistol**	Lady from Bristol
	Scabby Eye	**Pitch**	Hedge & Ditch
	Smack in the Eye	**Plant**	Uncle & Aunt
Pig	Lord Wig	**Plate**	Harry Tate
Pigeon	Merlin the Magician		One & Eight
Piles	Chalfont St Giles		Pearly Gate
	Farmer Giles	**Play**	Night & Day
	Nautical Miles	**Plug**	Little Brown Jug
	Nobby Stiles	**Po**	Jericho
	Seven Dials	**Pocket**	Chain & Locket
Pill(s)	Fanny Hill		Davy Crockett
	Jack & Jill		Lucy Locket
	Jenny Hill(s)		Sky Rocket
	Jimmy Hill(s)	**Poke**	Barney Moke
Pillow	Max Miller		Okey Doke
	Tit Willow		

Poker	Jolly Joker		Knox
	Orinoko		Royal Docks
Pole	Sausage Roll		Shoes & Socks
Poll (Head)	Sausage Roll		Surrey Docks
			Tilbury Docks
Ponce	Alphonse	**Pram**	Jar of Jam
	Candle & Sconce	**Pratt**	Top Hat
	Charlie Ronce		Trilby Hat
	Joe Ronce	**Prawn**	Frankie Vaughan
Pong	Anna May Wong	**Prayer**	Chocolate Eclair
	Hong Kong	**Price**	Snow Ice
Pony(£25)	Macaroni	**Price(s)**	Nits & Lice(s)
Poof (Homosexual)		**Prick (Penis)**	
	Horse's Hoof		Dipstick
	Iron Hoof		Hampton Wick
Poor	On the Floor		Joy Stick
Pope	Bar of Soap		Kiss Me Quick
Pork	Duchess of York		Sugar Stick
	Knife & Fork	**Prune**	Rangoon
Port (Wine)	Didn't Ought	**Psychiatrist**	Trick Cyclist
	Long & Short	**Pub**	Rub-a-Dub-Dub
	Pimple & Wart	**Puff (Breath)**	
Porter	Liffey Water		Nellie Duff
Portuguese	Pork & Beans	**Puff (Homosexual)**	
Poseur	Bulldozer		Collar & Cuff
	Carl Rosa		Nice Enough
Post	Holy Ghost	**Pull**	John Bull
	Tea & Toast	**Pump**	Skip & Jump
Pot	Sir Walter Scott	**Punter**	Billy Bunter
Potato	Navigator		Guzunter
	Spanish Waiter		Hillman Hunter
Potty	Mazawatee	**Push**	Bull & Bush
Pound	Hole in the Ground		Shepherd's Bush
	Lost & Found	**Putter**	Bread & Butter
	Merry Go Round	**Pyjamas**	Panoramas
Pox (VD)	Cardboard Box		
	Coachman on the Box	**Quaker**	Muffin Baker
	Dairy Box	**Quarter**	Mother & Daughter
	East India Docks	**Quasimodo**	Soda (Water)
	Jack in the Box	**Quay**	Robert E Lee
	Nervo & Knox		
	Reverend Ronald		

Queen (Playing Card)	
	Mary Green
Queen	Baked Bean
	Seldom Seen
Queer (Homosexual)	
	Nellie Dean
	Brighton Pier
	Ginger Beer
	King Lear
Queue	Pot of Glue
Quid	Saucepan Lid
	Tea Pot Lid
Races	Belt & Braces
Racket	Fag Packet
Rain	All Complain
	Andy Cain
	France & Spain
	Pleasure & Pain
Ramp	Postage Stamp
Randy	Port & Brandy
Rat	Bowler Hat
	Cocked Hat
Rates	Garden Gates
Razor	House of Fraser
Ready(s)	Nelson Eddy(s)
Red	Bald Head
Reg	Meat & Two Veg
Rent	Burton on Trent
	Duke of Kent
Rice	Rats & Mice
	Three Blind Mice
Ricket (Mistake)	
	Raffle Ticket
Right (correct)	
	Harbour Light
Right	Isle of Wight
Ring (Anus)	
	Pearly King
Ring	Ting-a-Ling

Risk It	Garibaldi Biscuit
River	Bullock's Liver
	Shake & Shiver
Road	Frog & Toad
Rocks	Salford Docks
Rod (Gun)	Tommy Dodd
Rofe	French Loaf
Roll	Nat King Cole
Room	Birch Broom
	Bride & Groom
	Shovel & Broom
Rope	Bar of Soap
Rotten	Billy Cotton
	Dolly Cotton
	Needle & Cotton
	Reels of Cotton
Round	Fox & Hound
	Hare & Hound
Row	Bull & Cow
Royals	Castor Oils
Ruck (Fight)	
	Dog & Duck
Rum	Finger & Thumb
	Thimble & Thumb
	Tom Thumb
Rumble	Come a Tumble
	Jerry-Cum-Mumble
Run	Currant Bun
	Hot Cross Bun
Runs (Diarrhoea)	
	Radio Ones
Sack (Dismissal)	
	Last Card in the Pack
	Pedlars Pack
Sack	Tin Tack
Saloon Bar	Balloon Car
Salt	Earls Court
	Hampton Court
	Squad Halt

Sandal(s)	Roman Candle(s)
Sauce	Rocking Horse
Saucer	Geoffrey Chaucer
Saveloy	Girl & Boy
	Myrna Loy
Savoury Rissole	
	Piss Hole
Saw	Denis Law
	Mother-in-Law
Say	First of May
Say So	Coffee & Cocoa
	Tea & Cocoa
Scarf	One & Half
	Tin Bath
Score	Apple Core
Scotch	Gold Watch
	Pimple & Blotch
Scouse	Mickey Mouse
Scout	Brussels Sprout
	Tea Grout
Scran	Tommy O'Rann
Scratch	Brands Hatch
Screw (Prison Officer)	
	Kangaroo
	Little Boy Blue
Sea	Coffee & Tea
	Housemaid's Knee
Seat	Boiled Sweet
See	Cup of Tea
Sense	Eighteen Pence
	Pounds & Pence
	Shillings & Pence
Serpentine	Turpentine
Seven	God in Heaven
Sex	Oedipus Rex
	Shell Mex
	T Rex
Shade (Sunglasses)	
	Jack of Spade

Shag (Coitus)	
	Melvyn Bragg
Shakes	Currant Cakes
	Rattle Snakes
Shaky	Currant Cakie
Shandy	Amos & Andy
	Andy Pandy
	Beano & Dandy
	Mahatma Gandhi
Share(s)	Rupert Bear(s)
Shave	Chas & Dave
	Dig in the Grave
	Misbehave
	Ocean Wave
Shed	King's Head
Shell	Heaven & Hell
Shelter	Helter Skelter
Sherry	Derry Down Derry
	Londonderry
	Woolwich Ferry
Shice	Block of Ice
Shilling	John Dillon
	Rogue & Villain
	Thomas Tilling
Shiner (Black Eye)	
	Morris Minor
	Ocean Liner
Ship	Halfpenny Dip
	Old Whip
Shirker	Office Worker
Shirt	Dicky Dirt
	Uncle Bert
Shit	Hard Hit
Shit(s)	Eartha Kitt(s)
	Edgar Britt(s)
	Two Bob Bit(s)
Shits	Jimmy Brits
	Nicker Bits
	Tom Tits
	Zazu Pitts
Shixa	Flour Mixer

Shoe	How D'ye Do	**Sister**	Blackman Kissed 'Er
Shoe(s)	One(s) & Two(s)		Bubble & Blister
Shoes	Bottle of Booze		Skin & Blister
	Canoes	**Six**	Chop Sticks
	Ps & Qs		Pick Up Sticks
	St Louis Blues		Tom Mix
Shonker (Nose)		**Skint**	Boracic Lint
	Beezonker		Pink Lint
Shooter (Gun)		**Skive**	Duck & Dive
	Phil the Fluter	**Skiver**	Screwdriver
Shop	Lollipop	**Sky**	Apple Pie
	Mrs Mopp		Shepherd's Pie
Short	Magistrate's Court	**Slash (Urinate)**	
Shoulder	Burn & Smoulder		J Carroll Naish
	Granite Boulder		Johnny Cash
Shoulder(s)	Rock(s) & Boulder(s)		Pie & Mash
Shout	Boy Scout	**Sleep**	Bo Peep
Shove It	Lord Lovat	**Slipper**	Jack the Ripper
Shovel	Lord Lovel	**Slippers**	Yorkshire Rippers
Shower	Bag of Flour	**Smack**	Uncle Mack
	Eiffel Tower	**Smell**	Heaven & Hell
	Eisenhower		William Tell
Shrimp	Colonel Blimp	**Smeller (Nose)**	
Shunter	Billy Bunter		Cinderella
Sick	Moby Dick	**Smile**	Crocodile
	Spotted Dick		River Nile
	Tom & Dick	**Smoke**	Laugh & Joke
	Tom, Harry & Dick		Old Oak
	Uncle Dick	**Smokes (Cigarettes)**	
Sidney	Steak & Kidney		Ash & Oaks
Sight	Flash of Light	**Snack**	Last Card in the Pack
Silly	Auntie Lilly	**Snake**	George Blake
	Daffadown Dilly	**Sneeze**	Bread & Cheese
	Piccadilly	**Snide**	Jeckyl & Hyde
	Uncle Willy		Mr Hyde
Sing	Highland Fling	**Snitch**	Wicked Witch
Sing(er)	Mangle & Wringer	**Snooker**	Bazooka
Sing Song	Ding Dong	**Snore/Snoring**	
Sip (Urinate)			Lions Roar(ing)
	Apple & Pip		Rain(ing) & Pour(ing)

Snot (Nasal Mucus)		
	Pease Pudding Hot	
Snout	In & Out	
	Salmon & Trout	
Snow	Buck & Doe	
	Come & Go	
	To & Fro	
Snuff	Harry Bluff	
	Lal Brough	
Soap	Band of Hope	
	Bob Hope	
	Cape of Good Hope	
	Charlie Pope	
Socks	Almond Rocks	
	Peppermint Rocks	
	Tilbury Docks	
Sod	Fillet of Cod	
	Haddock & Cod	
	Tommy Dodd	
Son/Sun	Bath Bun	
	Currant Bun	
	Hot Cross Bun	
	Penny Bun	
	Pie & One	
	Sticky Bun	
Sore(s)	Dudley Moore(s)	
Sot (Drunkard)		
	Piss Pot	
Sovereign	Jimmy O'Goblin	
Spade	Lemonade	
	Lucozade	
	Razor Blade	
Spanner	Elsie Tanner	
	Wheezy Anna	
Sparks (Electrician)		
	Groucho Marx	
Sparrow	Bow & Arrow	
Spats	Wanstead Flats	
Speak	Bubble & Squeak	
Spick	Oil Slick	
Spider	Apple Cider	

	Sit Beside Her
Spinach	Charlton & Greenwich
	Woolwich &
	Greenwich
Splinter	Harold Pinter
Spoon	Blue Moon
	High Noon
	Lorna Doone
Spot	Randolph Scott
Spot(s)	Selina Scott(s)
Spruce (Deceive)	
	Madam De Luce
Spud(s)	Rosebud(s)
Spunk (Semen)	
	Harry Monk
	Maria Monk
	Thelonius Monk
	Victoria Monk
Spy	Collar & Tie
Squirrel	Nice One Cyril
Stage	Birdcage
	Greengage
	Handley Page
Stairs	Apples & Pairs
	Stocks & Shares
	Trouble & Cares
Stake	Joe Blake
Stale	British Rail
Stall	Bat & Ball
Stalls	Niagara Falls
Start	Horse & Cart
State (of Agitation)	
	Harry Tate
	Six & Eight
	Two & Eight
Station	Constipation
	Poor Relation
	Salvation
Stays	Bryant & Mays
Steak	Joe Blake

Steel	Fillet of Veal	**Sure**	Five to Four
Stever	Coal Heaver	**Survive**	Duck & Dive
Stew	Boys in Blue	**Swab**	Couple o' Bob
	How D'ye Do	**Swear**	Lord Mayor
	Waterloo		Rip & Tear
Stink	Food & Drink	**Sweetheart**	Jam Tart
	Kitchen Sink	**Syph(ilis)**	Fighting Fifth
	Pen & Ink		Lover's Tiff
Stinker	Pen & Inker		Wills Whiff
Stir (Prison)	Ben Hur		
	Joe Gurr	**Table**	Betty Grable
Stockings	Reelings & Rockings		Cain Abel
	Silas Hockings		Clark Gable
Stooge	Moulin Rouge	**Taff**	Riff Raff
Stool	April Fools	**Tail**	Daily Mail
Story	Jackanory		Hammer & Nail
Stout	Salmon & Trout	**Tail (Prostitute)**	
Straight	Six & Eight		Brass Nail
Strain	Ball & Chain	**Tailor**	Popeye the Sailor
Stranger	Glasgow Ranger		Sinbad the Sailor
Stranger(s)	Queen's Park	**Tale**	Binnie Hale
	Ranger(s)		Daily Mail
Street	Field of Wheat		Hill & Dale
Strike Me Dead			Newgate Jail
	Bread		Weep & Wail
Stripper	Herring & Kipper	**Talk**	Duke of York
Strop (Masturbate)			Rabbit & Pork
	Whip & Top		Roast Pork
Strop(ping) (Masturbating)		**Talker**	Johnny Walker
	Christmas Shop(ping)	**Tan**	Desperate Dan
Stuff It	Little Miss Muffet	**Tanner (£10)**	
Style	Tate & Lyle		Goddess Diana
Sub	Rub-a-Dub-Dub		Lord of the Manor
Sub(s)	Rhubarb(s)		Sprasi Anna
Suit	Piccolo & Flute		Tartan Banner
	Whistle & Flute	**Tap (Borrow)**	
Sun	Old Jamaica Rum		Andy Capp
Supper	Tommy Tupper		Cellar Flap
		Tart	Exchange & Mart
		Tash (Moustache)	
			Dot & Dash

	Whip & Lash
Tasty	Cornish Pasty
Tax	Beeswax
Tea	Bug & Flea
	Jenny Lee
	Nancy Lee
	River Lea
	Rosie Lee
	You & Me
Teacher	Constant Screacher
Teeth	Bexley Heath
	Blackheath
	Edward Heath
	Hampstead Heath
	Hounslow Heath
	Roast Beef
	Ted Heath
Telephone	Jelly Bone
Telly	Custard & Jelly
	Marie Corelli
	Mother Kelly
	Ned Kelly
Ten	Big Ben
	Cock & Hen
	Cockerel & Hen
Tenner (£10)	Ayrton Senna
Thick (Stupid)	Paddy & Mick
Thief	Autumn Leaf
	Corned Beef
	Edward Heath
	Leg of Beef
	Tea Leaf
	Ted Heath
Thin	Needle & Pin
Three	Dearie Me
Throat	Nanny Goat
Throne	Rag & Bone
Thrush	Basil Brush
Thumb	Jamaica Rum

Thunder	Stand From Under
Ticket	Bat & Wicket
	Leg Before Wicket
	Wilson Pickett
Tie	Butterfly
	Fourth of July
	Peckham Rye
	Pig's Fry
Tight	Black & White
	Box of Lights
	Fly By Night
	High as a Kite
	Isle of Wight
Tight(s)	Fly By Nights
	Snow Whites
Till	Jack & Jill
Time	Birdlime
	Harry Lime
	Lemon & Lime
Tinkle/Sprinkle (Urinate)	Rip Van Winkle
Tip (Gratuity)	Sherbet Dip
Tip(s)	Fish & Chip(s)
Tit(s)	Fainting Fit(s)
	Threepenny Bit(s)
Tits	Brace & Bits
	First Aid Kits
Tittie(s)	Town(s) & City(s)
Titty	Bristol City
	Capital City
	Manchester City
Toast	Holy Ghost
	Pig & Roast
Tobacco	Hi Jimmy Knacker
	Noser My Knacker
Toby	George Robey
Toe(s)	Sebastian Coe(s)
	Stop & Go(s)
Toes	Buttons & Bows
	These & Those

Tongue	Brewer's Bung
	Brother Bung
	Jimmy Young

Tonic (Water)
Philharmonic

| Tools | April Fools |
| | Crown Jewels |

| Tooth | Auntie Ruth |
| | General Booth |

| Torch | Back Porch |

| Tory | Fairy Story |

Toss (Masturbate)
Iron Horse
Joe Loss
Polish & Gloss
Stirling Moss
Victoria Cross

| Tote | Canal Boat |
| | Nanny Goat |

Tout	Brussels Sprout
	In & Out
	Salmon & Trout

Towel	Enoch Powell
	Mortar & Trowel
	Sandy Powell
	William Powell

Town	Jim Brown
	Joe Brown
	Mother Brown

| Toy | Girl & Boy |

Traffic Warden
Gay Gordon

| Train | Hail & Rain |
| | Struggle & Strain |

| Trainers | Struggle & Strainers |
| | Tea Strainers |

Tram	Baa Lamb
	Bread & Jam
	Jar of Jam

| Tramp | Halfpenny Stamp |

| Tray | Vicar of Bray |

| Trial | Over the Stile |

| Tricky | Ranjitiki |

| Tripe | Cherry Ripe |

Trots (Diarrhoea)
Red Hots
Zachary Scotts

Trotter(s) Feet
Gillie Potters

Trousers	Callard & Bowsers
	Council Houses
	Round the Houses

Trowel	Baden Powell
	Bark & Growl
	Enoch Powell

| True | Eyes of Blue |
| | Irish Stew |

| Truth | Dog's Tooth |
| | Maud & Ruth |

| Tube | Oxo Cube |

| Tumble | Jerry-Cum-Mumble |

| Tune | Stewed Prune |

Turd	Douglas Hurd
	George the Third
	My Word
	Richard the Third

| Turkey | Pinky & Perky |

| Turn | Butter Churn |

Twat (Vagina)
Glue Pot
Honey Pot
Mustard Pot

Twig (to scratch an itchy anus)
Gavel & Wig

Twig (to understand)
Earwig

| Twirls | Boys & Girls |

| Two | Dirty Old Jew |
| | Doctor Who |

| Tyre(s) | Dorothy Squire(s) |

Umbrella	Cousin Ella Isabella	**Wanker**	Casablanca Crown & Anchor Merchant Banker Oil Tanker
Uncle	Carbuncle	**Warder**	Harry Lauder
Undertaker	Overcoat Maker	**Warmer**	Daisy Dormer
Van	Peter Pan	**Wash**	Bob Squash Lemon Squash
Vest	Brigs Rest East & West Sunday Best Wild West	**Watch**	Bottle of Scotch Gordon & Gotch
Vicar	Half a Nicker Pie & Liquor	**Water**	Darling Daughter Dirty Daughter Fisherman's Daughter Mother & Daughter Ratcatcher's Daughter
Villain	Harold Macmillan		
Vin Blanc	Plink Plonk		
Voice	Hobson's Choice Housewives' Choice Rolls Royce Walter Joyce	**Way**	Doris Day Edna May
		Weak	Bubble & Squeak
		Weather	Hat & Feather
Volley	Buddy Holly	**Weed**	Oliver Reed
Wad	Ken Dodd	**Week**	Bubble & Squeak
Wages	Greengages Rock of Ages	**Weight**	Pieces of Eight Love & Hate
Waistcoat	Charlie Prescott Colonel Prescott Jim Prescott	**Weights**	Harry Tates
		West	Jacket & Vest
		Wheel(s)	Jellied Eel(s)
Waiter	Baked Potato Cold Potato Hot Potato Roast Potato	**Whip**	Tumble & Tip
		Whisky	Bright & Frisky Gay & Frisky I'm So Frisky
Walk	Ball of Chalk Penn'orth of Chalk Powdered Chalk	**Whistle**	Partick Thistle
		Whizz	Bottle of Fizz
Wall	Bat & Ball	**Whore**	Bolt the Door Jane Shore Six to Four Tug o' War
Wally	Buddy Holly		

Wank (Masturbate)
     Barclays Bank
     J Arthur Rank
     Levy & Frank
     Piggy Bank
     Sherman Tank
     Taxi Rank
		Wife	Carving Knife
			Duchess of Fife
			Kiss of Life
			Light of My Life
			Sporting Life

	Struggle & Strife	**Yard**	Bladder of Lard
	Trouble & Strife	**Yellow**	Cinderella
	War & Strife	**Yes**	Black Bess
	Worry & Strife		Brown Bess
Wig	Irish Jig	**Yid**	Front Wheel Skid
	Syrup of Fig		Saucepan Lid
Wild	Brown & Mild		Tea Pot Lid
Win	Nose & Chin		Tin Lid
Wind(y)	Jenny Lind(y)	**Yid(s)**	God Forbid(s)
Window	Burnt Cinder	**Young**	Well Hung
Window(s)	Polly Flinder(s)	**Yuppie**	Hush Puppy
Windy	Rawalpindi		
Wine	Rise & Shine		
	River Tyne		
Winkle(s)	Grannies Wrinkle		
Winner	Christmas Dinner		
	Hot Dinner		
Wish(es)	Pot(s) & Dish(es)		
Wog	Chocolate Frog		
	Hedgehog		
	Nig Nog		
Woman	Gooseberry Pudding		

Wood(s) (Woodbine)
　　　　　Do Me Good(s)
　　　　　Robin Hood(s)

Wop (Italian)
　　　　　Bottle of Pop
　　　　　Grocer's Shop

Word	Dicky Bird
	Early Bird
	Richard the Third
Work	Captain Kirk
	Dunkirk
	Smile & Smirk
	Terrible Turk
World	Flag Unfurled
Yank	Ham Shank
	Sherman Tank
	Wooden Plank
Yankee	Widow Twankey